the little book of etiquette

PATSY ROWE

the little book of etiquette

- ▸ Dating
- ▸ Eating
- ▸ Entertaining
- ▸ Introductions
- ▸ Mobile phones
- ▸ Weddings

NEW HOLLAND

First published in Australia in 2005 by
New Holland Publishers (Australia) Pty Ltd
Sydney • Auckland • London • Cape Town

1/66 Gibbes Street Chatswood NSW 2067 Australia
218 Lake Road Northcote Auckland New Zealand
86 Edgware Road London W2 2EA United Kingdom
80 McKenzie Street Cape Town 8001 South Africa

10 9 8 7 6 5 4 3

National Library of Australia Cataloguing-in-Publication Data:

Rowe, Patsy.
          The little book of etiquette.

          Includes index.
          ISBN 9781741102406 (pbk.).

          1. Etiquette. 2. Manners and customs. I. Title.

          395

Project Editor: Monica Barton
Designer: Joanne Buckley
Printer: Griffin Press, Adelaide

CONTENTS

INTRODUCTION

Etiquette is correct and acceptable behaviour that makes social contact run smoothly. Sometimes we find ourselves in situations for which we aren't prepared. This book aims to set you on the right path so that you can cope with any social situation with confidence.

Chapter 1
MEETING AND GREETING

When someone is being introduced to you, concentrate and *listen*; if you don't catch the name, ask for it to be repeated. It's important, whether in business or social circles, to get people's names right. If you use that person's name as soon as you can in conversation, you'll find it easier to remember.

WHAT IF YOU CAN'T RECALL SOMEONE'S NAME?

An awkward situation can occur when someone you know well, or perhaps someone you've met recently, recognises you and walks over to greet you—and you can't remember who they are. You have three options:

1. Hope they're wearing a nametag. If they aren't, you can say something like, 'What a surprise! What are you up to these days?', hoping the answer will jog your memory and give you time to remember their name.
2. If you can't possibly remember their name, then you're going to have to say, 'I'll have to get you to help me with your name ...' Of course, the person will say their first name and you can quickly reply, 'I remembered your first name, it was your surname that escaped me.' At least that way, people think you half remembered them and it just softens that awkward moment.
3. The only other way to avoid being found out is to keep up a running monologue until he or she either introduces themselves to the group (if you're in a group situation), or a group member offers their hand in introduction. Say, 'I'm great with faces but terrible with names—I have to confess yours has gone right out of my head at the moment.'

WHAT IF YOUR NAME HAS BEEN FORGOTTEN?

If someone is introducing you and forgets your name, smile and help them out by saying it clearly. If you walk up to someone at a function to speak to them, you should say your name as you extend your arm to shake hands. This saves them the possible embarrassment of trying to remember your name, especially if they have to introduce you to the other people in the group.

Sometimes you may be introduced to others by the wrong name; there's no need to be embarrassed, just tell the person making the introduction that your name is 'Rowe' not 'Rose' and that you're Peter's sister, not his wife. Just say, 'Sorry, but I just thought I'd let you know that ...'

WHO MAKES INTRODUCTIONS?

Both hosts (if there is more than one host, for example, husband and wife) should introduce guests. If you're in charge of organising a function for someone else, then you should regard yourself as playing the role of host and make introductions. The correct responses for all introductions are: 'How do you do' or 'How are you?'

The rationale behind a good introduction is:

• to give each person the name of the other and a 'tag' of information that helps to initiate a conversation

• to put people at ease and to create an air of immediate friendliness and warmth so that conversation can flourish

• to lay the groundwork to avoid any embarrassment or misunderstanding.

USING TAGS

Introductions often lead into a conversation if a 'tag' is used. A 'single tag' is something said about the person being introduced while a 'double tag' tells you something about both parties.

A single tag is, for example: 'Mary, I'd like you to meet Peter Black who has just arrived from New York for Judy and Brian's wedding next week.' Mary now knows who Peter is, where he's from and why he's visiting. If you have to leave her to greet another guest, she and Peter can go on with some conversation about New York, the flight over, or how he came to know Judy and Brian.

A double tag is, for example: 'Mary, I'd like you to meet Peter Black who has just arrived from New York for Judy and Brian's wedding next week. Mary and her husband Tom lived in New York for 10 years when Tom was studying geology at the New York State University.' By saying something about both Mary and Tom, they can still talk about Peter, but they have the choice of discussing their years in New York, his research at the university, and how New York has changed. There will be no awkward silences until you return to talk to them, or other people join their group.

Situation 1
The younger person, or lowest ranking, is introduced first to the older person or highest ranking, e.g. 'Professor Stevenson, I'd like you to meet one of my students, Susan Black.'

Situation 2
The man is always introduced to the woman and you should always say the woman's name first, e.g. 'Judy, I've been wanting you to meet Peter Morris ...'

Situation 3
If you're introducing a married couple with different surnames, or a couple to a single person, you should introduce the man to the woman, and then to her husband or partner, e.g. 'Simon, I'd like you to meet Karen O'Keefe and her husband/partner Bob Brown.'

WHEN TO SHAKE HANDS?

Both men and women shake hands with one another but in certain situations, it's correct for the more senior or higher-ranking person to offer their hand first. For instance, if you were invited to meet the Governor-General, you wouldn't thrust your hand out, but pause until the Governor-General made a move.

A handshake should be firm so that the hands meet palm-to-palm; not by clasping at a person's fingers. Your hand should be perpendicular to the ground rather than rolled over sideways.

WHEN TO KISS

If you know someone well, you may prefer to kiss upon meeting and farewelling. This should only be a kiss on the cheek, however, or perhaps the European 'double kiss' (one on each cheek), or if you really like someone the 'triple kiss' (left, right and left cheek again).

How passionate should you be in public?

Not too passionate! Public displays of affection are embarrassing for those who know you—and for those who don't. A kiss on the cheek, or on the lips (but not for too long), holding hands, hugging, and walking arm-in-arm are all fine, but lingering kisses accompanied by heavy breathing and wandering hands are definitely unacceptable.

WHEN TO STAND?

It's sensible for men and women to stand when new guests are arriving so that handshaking is more comfortable. If women prefer not to shake hands, or the group is very big, they should remain seated. Standing for an older or higher-ranking person is always courteous.

In a restaurant

In a restaurant, a person doesn't need to stand up if someone he or she knows walks past their table, but if the acquaintance were to stop and start a conversation, it would be more comfortable for him or her to stand so they can speak and shake hands at the same level. Conversation should be brief so that other guests are not neglected, nor meals left to get cold.

Common courtesies on public transport

Able-bodied men and women should rise and offer their seats to the elderly, disabled or heavily pregnant. Most women still appreciate chivalry and will be delighted if a man offers his seat. However, some women may dislike this gesture, so men need to use their intuition.

Whoever reaches a door first should open it and the person nearest the elevator door should exit first.

Assisting with carrying heavy or cumbersome objects can be done by either sex. When helping others to seat themselves, males and females should help elderly or incapacitated guests pull a heavy dining chair out from the table and should also push it back in again once the person is seated. The same applies to helping someone put on a coat or jacket.

If someone's fly is undone or they have lipstick on their teeth or they have spinach lodged between their front teeth, tell them so with tact. If, however, someone has bad body odour or bad breath, you can bring it up by saying, 'I don't know if you've changed your deodorant but you smell different' if you know them well, or you can offer them a mint and say, 'I don't know about you, but I find my breath is much better when I suck on one of these from time to time.'

WHEN TO SAY 'PLEASE', 'THANK YOU', 'EXCUSE ME', 'I BEG YOUR PARDON' AND 'I'M SORRY'

Any request should be preceded by 'please' and when the request is completed, answered with 'thank you'. 'Excuse me' is used when you want to walk in front of someone, reach for something, break into a group conversation, or ask a question. 'I beg your pardon' or sometimes just 'Pardon' is said when you don't hear what someone has said and you would like them to repeat it. Apologising is also an important part of social interaction and if you make a *faux pas*, or false step (which hopefully you won't after reading this book), you must apologise immediately with 'I'm sorry'. If you bump into someone, tread on their toes, cause them to drop something or misunderstand something they say, you should say, 'I'm sorry ...'

GIVING AND RECEIVING COMPLIMENTS

It's polite to compliment your host/s for their hospitality or a friend who has a new hairstyle. Make sure your compliment is simple and genuine. When you receive a compliment, show you're pleased and accept it graciously by saying, 'thank you'. Avoid being dismissive by saying such things as, 'Oh, this old dress. I've never worn red. I don't know why I bought it really!' as you'll make the person who admired it feel embarrassed.

Chapter 2

SENDING AND RECEIVING INVITATIONS

You can invite people to any function by a telephone call, or you can simply drop them a line—both methods have advantages and disadvantages and much will depend on the formality of the occasion. The clear advantage of a note or formal card is that it states the day, time, dress code and the address—all of which can be a problem if the invitation is more casually extended over the telephone.

Avoid sending out invitations too far in advance, unless you're prepared to do a quick ring around a week or so before to jog memories.

THREE TIPS FOR MAXIMISING SHOW-UPS

If there's a guest of honour, before sending out the written or printed invitations, contact that person to check the suitability of the date you've chosen.

If it's important to have a certain group of attend (for instance, at an engagement party where you want parents from both sides of the two families to be present), ring the main players first to make sure the date you've chosen suits them. The written invitation then serves as a reminder.

Send out invitations for special functions three to four weeks before the date of the function.

WHAT TO DO WHEN YOU RECEIVE AN INVITATION

If you receive an informal invitation, reply quickly as the person hosting the function needs to know the numbers for catering and, secondly, there are probably others they would like to invite if you're unable to attend. If the invitation has RSVP (*répondez s'il vous plaît*—

'reply if you please') the bottom, a date will appear beside it—this is the latest date at which the invitation can be answered. If the RSVP provides a phone number, then you may reply by telephone. This is the time to check on the correct address, time and dress for the occasion.

If you receive a formal written invitation, the correct way to reply is in writing by repeating the facts given on the invitation with words or phrases to link them.

SENDING INVITATIONS

Invitations should be sent with enough time for people to respond. The RSVP time frame varies with the type of function being held.

Invitation to a dinner party

Invite people by written letter, telephone or email two to three weeks before you would like to hold the function, and be prepared to juggle dates. Once a set date has been reached, confirm it with the time of arrival and dress code. At the same time, check if any of the guests has any particular dietary requirements.

Invitation to a cocktail party

Invite people by written letter, telephone or email two to three weeks before you would like to hold the function, and again be prepared to juggle dates. Once a set date has been reached, confirm it with the time of arrival and dress code.

Cocktail parties often have a finishing time, so make sure you specify this with the invitation. Make sure the finishing time on the invitation is half an hour earlier than you plan, so that you won't have people overstay their welcome.

Invitation to a house-warming party

Invite people by written letter, telephone or email a few weeks ahead and be specific about the date, time and new address. It is acceptable to ask people to bring alcohol. If guests ask if they may bring a gift, don't suggest anything expensive; suggest something small and inexpensive such as herbs for a planned herb garden or fragrant soap for the bathroom.

Invitation to a christening

Invite people by written leter, telephone or email. The priest, minister or rabbi who performs the ceremony (and their spouse) is usually invited to the party afterwards, if there is to be one. If you only want a small gathering, then only invite the godparents, family and close friends.

WHAT IF YOU SEND AN INVITATION BUT RECEIVE NO RESPONSE?

If you've put a date on your RSVP, ring two days before that date to confirm that the invitation did arrive and to ask if it will be accepted. Two days are necessary because it may take you some time to get hold of your prospective guest, and if you find they're not coming it gives you time to invite someone else and to confirm catering numbers.

If you can't contact the person you wish to invite either at home, at work, or through neighbours, friends or offspring, assume they are not coming and invite someone else.

If you invite someone else and then hear from the first guests a few days before your function and after the RSVP date, it's quite reasonable to explain your dilemma and that you have invited someone else. If you're still able to, you may wish to arrange extra places for them; if not, assure them they're first on the list for the next get-together.

If your function is a stand-up cocktail party or casual barbecue, it won't matter if you have two extra guests.

WEDDING INVITATIONS

Since the bride's parents are officially the hosts of their daughter's wedding, the invitations go out in their name. If they're deceased or divorced then the invitation goes out in the name of the person who has taken the role of host. If the bride's parents are divorced and have little contact, the invitation should go out in the name of the parent who has adopted the role of host; for instance, if the mother of the bride has remarried, the invitation should go out in her married name. If the mother is widowed, then the invitation should go out in her widowed name.

If the couple is being married overseas and will be hosting their own wedding, then the invitation should go out in their names, e.g. John Smith and Mary Carruthers.

If the bridegroom's parents have taken it upon themselves to host the wedding, then the invitation would go out in their name.

If both the bride and bridegroom have had previous marriages and only a small number of people are invited to the second wedding, the bride and bridegroom would contact the guests personally through a note or telephone call.

If parents of both the bride and groom are sharing the wedding costs, place both names on the invitation, with the names of the bride's parents first. Either the mother of the bride can post out all the invitations and handle the replies, or the invitation list can be divided, with each side of the family sending out those invitations to their friends and family and be responsible for chasing up those replies.

Invitations should be sent approximately six to eight weeks before the wedding.

Nine parts of a formal wedding invitation

All wedding invitations need to contain nine pieces of very important information:

1. The hosts' names.
2. The invitation itself ('request the company of ...').
3. Who is being married.
4. The location of the wedding ceremony.
5. The date.
6. The time.
7. The location of the reception.
8. Instructions for replying to the invitation.
9. Dress code.

Wedding invitations are invariably printed. There are several reasons for this: there is a lot of information to impart and it would take a long time to give this out verbally; there is always the danger of being misheard, misunderstood or omitting to mention something in a verbal invitation, and the guest can pin the invitation up and take it with them on the day to check the address and time. Below is a sample wedding invitation.

SAMPLE FORMAL WEDDING INVITATION

Mr and Mrs John White
request the pleasure of your company
at the wedding of their daughter
Meredith Jane
to
James Anthony Perkins
at St Marks Church
Darling Point

on Wednesday, 16th July, 20XX
at 6.00 p.m.

and afterwards at
The Royal Motor Yacht Club
16 Smith Street
Point Piper
at 8.00 p.m.

RSVP 30th June, 20XX
2117 The Crest
Castle Cove NSW 1632
Black Tie

SAMPLE REPLY FOR FORMAL WEDDING INVITATION

Anthony and Mary Smith
have pleasure in accepting
the invitation of
Mr and Mrs John White
to attend the wedding of their daughter
Meredith Jane
to
James Anthony Perkins
at St Marks Church
Darling Point

on Wednesday, 16th July, 20XX
at 6.00 p.m.

and afterwards at
The Point Piper Yacht Club
16 Smith Street
Point Piper
At 8.00 p.m.

SAMPLE INFORMAL WEDDING INVITATION

William and Mary Smith would be delighted if you could attend
the wedding of their daughter, Margaret, to Anthony Johnson at
St Mark's Church, Ascot, on
Wednesday, 16 July 20XX at 6.00 p.m.
RSVP 2 July 20XX
(02) 5555 1234
Lounge Suit

If the invitation requests that you 'and guest/partner' attend, you should tell the host whether you *will* or *won't* be bringing someone. You should also give the host the name of your guest/partner so the host is able to both greet them and introduce them to other guests.

If you've been invited to come alone, but wish to bring a newly-acquired partner, you must ask the host. Never attend a function with an uninvited guest.

Many invitations come with a reply card included which you should use.

For all invitations, if you can't go you should still reply using the method given with the RSVP.

Sample divorced parents' wedding invitation

These days with many couples having divorced and re-married, the invitation should give the names of both parents. If the woman has re-married, her current married name is used.

New partners of the hosting parent/s will be invited depending on the interpersonal relationships of both the bride or bridegroom with the step-parent. If the relationship is poor, it may be preferable to hold a pre-wedding dinner for step-parents, and not include them at the wedding itself.

SAMPLE DIVORCED PARENTS' WEDDING INVITATION

William Smith and Mary Forsythe
would be delighted if you could join them
to celebrate the wedding
of their daughter, Maggie, to Tony Johnson
in the garden of the Boathouse by the Lake,
on Wednesday, 16th July, 20XX at 11.00 a.m.

RSVP
30th June, 20XX
(02) 5555 1234
Smart casual
Champagne and canapés will be served

For more information on engagement and wedding etiquette, see chapters 7 and 8.

Chapter 3

DINNER PARTIES AT HOME AND AWAY

Dinner parties are events where you can impress your friends and family with your culinary skills and sense of style and presentation. When entertaining others, it can be rewarding to put in more effort than usual, while making it all appear effortless! The trick is to be well organised.

The experienced host will allow a reasonable margin of lateness for guests, although a socially acceptable lateness of twenty minutes would be about as much as any meal would stand. Remember too, that those guests who did arrive at the requested time will already have had at least one pre-dinner drink. Hosts shouldn't ply their guests with too much alcohol before dinner, and after forty-five minutes guests should go to the table and begin the meal. Late arrivals should join in at whatever course is being served.

When you realise that you're not going to make the function on time, ring immediately and forewarn the host that you'll be late and try to give an estimate of when you will arrive.

The first thing a guest should do is greet the host on arrival. It's also a thoughtful gesture to take a gift when going to someone's home, for instance, a bottle of wine, a jar of jam, mustard or olives, flowers or scented soap. If the occasion is to celebrate the birth of a new baby, take a gift for the baby; if your hosts have just added a billiard room, take a gift relevant to that room. Similarly, if you know that your hosts are about to go overseas take a relevant gift, such as a currency exchange calculator.

GIFTS FOR LUNCH OR DINNER INVITATIONS

There is no rule about taking a gift for your host or hostess when you visit their home, but it's a thoughtful gesture and shows you really appreciate being invited.

What to take if you're a man going alone

If you're a man attending a lunch or dinner alone, the following gifts are appropriate:

- flowers—if you're concerned about your host needing to arrange them while other guests are arriving, make sure it's a fixed arrangement, or take a pot plant
- exotic teas or coffees
- a bottle of wine, champagne, port or liqueur
- a book, magazine or video you know your host would enjoy
- a 'hobby' gift—trout 'flies' for him, monogrammed golf tees for her.

What to take if you're a woman going alone

If you're a woman attending a lunch or dinner alone, the following gifts are appropriate:

- any of the above (if a woman takes wine or champagne, it's more elegant to tie a ribbon around it or present it in a pretty wine bag).
- a basket of mini jams, chutney, relish, nuts or herb vinegar
- perfumed or floating candles
- toiletries such as bath oil, soaps or talcum powder.

It's important not to embarrass anyone by giving an expensive gift which they will feel they can't match when they visit you, and which makes the gifts of the other guests seem paltry.

Try to open the gift in front of the giver so that they gain pleasure from your pleasure and even if it's something you know you'll never use, eat, drink or be able to give away, look pleased and say something nice about it and, of course, say 'thank you'. If you have a gift shelf where you store gifts you don't like or have no use for, make sure you put a label on them noting who they're from. It's very poor etiquette giving back a gift to the person who gave it to you! If the gift is from a friend or relative who visits you regularly, then keep it handy so you can put it in the hallway or on a shelf when he or she visits.

WHAT TO WEAR

When replying to a dinner invitation, ask whether the meal is indoors or outdoors—and what the hostess will be wearing as 'come casual' can be misleading. Men can always ask, 'Will John be wearing a tie and jacket?'

What is 'black tie' and when to wear it?

'Black tie' means a men's black dinner suit with matching trousers and jacket. Today men have become more adventurous, so coloured bow ties and matching cummerbund and waistcoat have become popular. Black tie is worn to balls, some weddings, formal dinners, banquets and presentations. In warmer climates, a white jacket called a tuxedo replaces the more formal black jacket.

A woman may vary what she wears according to the formality of the function. For instance, a short cocktail or dinner dress can be worn to a dinner or wedding, a mid-calf dress to a more formal wedding, or a full-length dress to a ball. Some women even prefer to wear evening pants.

What is 'lounge suit' or 'jacket and tie' and when to wear it?

This is a regular day suit with matching pants and jacket and a long-sleeved shirt and tie. This could be worn for a dinner in someone's home, a formal luncheon, a christening, a funeral, a wedding or a job interview.

For a woman, it will depend on the nature of the occasion as women may wear a cocktail dress, a black dress, a pantsuit, a dress and a jacket, or a skirt and jacket, or even long flowing pants.

TIPS FOR EASY, ELEGANT ENTERTAINING AT HOME

Start planning your occasion about three weeks in advance by ensuring you have a good mix of 'talkers' and 'non-talkers' and when telephoning to invite your guests, ask about any dietary restrictions. Whether inviting by telephone or written note, you should mention the day, date, time and place (indoors or outdoors), and give guests an idea of what to wear and if the dinner party is to celebrate anything special.

If you have children or pets it's only natural that you adore them, but remember that some of your guests may not be so enthusiastic. You should ask guests whether they like dogs or cats before they enter your house. That way you can keep your pets away from guests if you find that they're either scared of them or allergic to them. If you have children, it's best to have the dinner party later so they've been put to bed, or organise a quiet activity to keep them interested until their bedtime. Dinner parties and children seldom mix.

After the event, keep a list of who you've invited and what you served so you avoid asking the same combination of friends again, or serving the identical meal.

If you're invited to a dinner party, luncheon or barbecue at someone's home you should reply promptly, especially if you can't attend, so that someone else can be invited.

The 'count-down'

Whether you've just moved into your new home and are entertaining for the first time, or the children have grown up and moved out and you're starting all over again, keep any entertaining simple and do as much in advance as possible. Helpful hints include:

- shop in advance
- polish the silver
- put mixers (dry ginger, tonic water, soda water etc), wine, champagne, beer and soft drink in the refrigerator
- order ice
- fill condiment containers with salt and pepper, mustard etc, and toothpick holders
- prepare the dessert, soup or entrée two days beforehand—this leaves you with just the main course and nibbles to prepare on the day
- set the table two days before
- place handtowels and soap in the toilet to be used by guests
- arrange flowers the day before.

If you need to buy fresh flowers, you can weave magic by filling out with greenery to make them go further.

Menu preparation

Keep it simple and serve dishes you've cooked before that can, preferably, be prepared days in advance.

You should also take into consideration the balance of the meal; serving too many creamy foods together can overload the palate and will leave your guests feeling bloated. If you prepare a very rich main dish, ensure that you serve steamed vegetables or a simple salad with a light dressing as an accompaniment.

Tips for table decoration

Be wary of placing highly-scented flowers on the table as their fragrance can activate allergies as well as overpower the smell of the food being served.

Keep all decorations, flowers and drip-free candles low to avoid blocking eye contact across the table.

Make sure that there are plenty of containers of black pepper, salt or other condiments you need to go with the meal.

How to lay the table

When setting the table for a dinner party, use your imagination in your use of colour, china, cutlery and candles etc, but avoid cluttering the table with unnecessary dinnerware. There should be plenty of space for food to be served and drinks to be poured.

Tablecloths

Tablecloths or tablemats can be used, but if you have a very beautiful table that you want to protect, use either a heat-resistant cloth (or a blanket) with your tablecloth over it, or cloth placemats with heat-resistant mats on top.

Cutlery setting

Each place at the table has its own complete setting for each course, beginning with the first course setting, usually on the outside. You start eating from the outside and work inwards finishing with the cutlery nearest to the plate for the last course, which is usually dessert or cheese.

Knives should be laid with the blade facing inwards and the spoons and forks should face upwards. All cutlery should go on the appropriate side of the dinner plate (knives and spoons on the right and forks on the left), but if you're short of space, then the butter knife may go north to south on the side plate (bread and butter plate), which is on the left of the place setting. Dessert spoons and dessert forks can be placed above the place setting with the spoon on the top and the handle to the right; the fork is placed below the dessert spoon with the handle on the left.

If you are left-handed, leave your cutlery in the right-handed position when you finish each course.

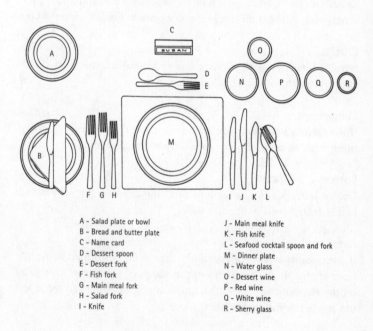

A – Salad plate or bowl
B – Bread and butter plate
C – Name card
D – Dessert spoon
E – Dessert fork
F – Fish fork
G – Main meal fork
H – Salad fork
I – Knife

J – Main meal knife
K – Fish knife
L – Seafood cocktail spoon and fork
M – Dinner plate
N – Water glass
O – Dessert wine
P – Red wine
Q – White wine
R – Sherry glass

How to lay the table

Glasses

Glasses are placed to the right above the knives; ideally, there should be a different glass for each wine to be served and another glass for water. If you're short of glasses, you can rinse them out and re-use them. Other glasses, such as those for dessert wine, port, liqueur or cognac, can be brought to the table when required. With the exception of the dessert wineglass, which remains through the coffee, each glass is removed with the course it accompanies or when coffee is served at the table. If cheese is served, dessert wine may be replaced by port, which in most homes would probably be served in the same glass.

Napkins

Use plain cotton, linen or damask napkins, not paper, and fold napkins simply and lay them on top of the side plate to the left of the setting.

Cruets

Small containers with spoons (called cruets) are used to decant chutney, pickles, mustard, oil or vinegar.

Condiments

If the table is very long you may need more than one set of everything, such as salt and pepper shakers or cruets of mustard.

Butter or margarine

Decant butter or margarine into small dishes and serve with a small butter knife, spreader or mini fork.

Name cards

If name cards are being used, they should be positioned above the place setting. It can be useful to put the guest's name in large print on the back of the card so that guests sitting opposite can see it and use it when speaking to them.

Salad plates

You can either:

- bring salad plates or bowls to the table with the salad

- set a small side plate or bowl at the left of the placemat
- have a salad knife and fork as part of the 'line-up'. These would usually be placed on the inside (if salad were to be eaten after the main course), or to the right of the main meal cutlery (if salad is to be eaten before the main course).

How to seat your guests

Take the time to work out a seating plan for your guests so you don't have all the talkers competing with each other at one end of the table while silence reigns at the other. Guide people to where they are to sit at the table when dinner is about to be served or use place cards. Seating plans should:

- alternate men and women as far as possible
- seat a shy person next to a good talker
- seat the most important man on the *right of the hostess*; if that person has a partner, be it male or female, that person will be seated *on the right of the host*
- seat the second most important man on the *left of the hostess* and his partner on the *left of the host* (this arrangement follows for the rest of the table)
- seat a friend who is single, but would prefer not to be, next to someone eligible
- seat guests with similar interests together, for instance, two women who were both school principals before retiring, or two new young mothers who may want to swap baby stories. This works well if you have uneven numbers of men and women
- make sure your own chair gives you easy access to the kitchen.

COCKTAIL PARTIES OR INVITING PEOPLE IN FOR DRINKS

Cocktail parties or drinks are usually run from 5.30–6.00 p.m. until 7.30–8.00 p.m. If you intend to entertain outdoors, don't invite more people than you can accommodate indoors, should it rain.

Ring early enough to give people time to plan ahead. Make sure you give the day, date, time (for instance 6.00–8.00 p.m.) and dress code. Emphasise that the invitation is for 'drinks'; however, if you don't mind people staying on, have a fork dish in the crock-pot.

If you know that some of your friends are vague or disorganised, make a diary entry to ring and remind them a few days beforehand.

Don't offer too many dishes—stick to easily prepared food such as one hot hors d'oeuvre platter and small finger food that won't drip all over your carpet.

Have more glasses available than guests invited—people have a habit of putting a glass down, forgetting where they put it and taking a fresh one. Tie a thin piece of ribbon around the stem of your wineglass so that you know which glass is yours if you put it down.

Have plenty of paper napkins at the ready; ashtrays if you permit smoking inside; and plates scattered around for toothpicks left over from food served on skewers.

If you've invited quite a crowd, you may want to invest in a waiter. Some waiters serve food as well as alcohol and even arrange simple canapés, which can be very helpful.

As for how much alcohol to order (see 'Wine and drinks'), ask your local wine merchant if you can return any unused bottles.

If you have expensive or antique furniture, ensure you put out plenty of coasters to avoid careless guests leaving dewy glasses where they shouldn't or move furniture and/or rugs into rooms that guests won't be in.

What drinks to serve?
Choose beer, red and white wine, 'bubbly' and perhaps one cocktail you've pre-mixed made with fruit juice to keep the alcoholic content down (e.g. sparkling white wine with peach nectar; a mulled wine is inexpensive and delicious in winter months, or soft drink).

HOW TO HOST A SIT-DOWN DINNER
Sit-down dinner parties usually begin at 7:30 p.m. for 8:00 p.m. The number of guests you invite depends on your culinary skills, organisational ability, the size of your table and your glassware, china and cutlery.

What to serve?

If you serve a cold soup or entrée and a dessert, like a crème caramel, all of which can be made the day before, you're left with only the main course to do on the night. Cheese or fresh fruit can replace the dessert.

How to serve the meal

Platters of food can be served either on a side table or the dining table itself for guests to serve themselves, or meals can be plated individually in the kitchen and brought to the table ready to eat. At the end of each course unused wineglasses, gravy boats, salt and pepper containers etc should be removed but nothing should be removed while guests are still eating.

Coffee or tea, with chocolates or petits fours, can be served either at the table or in the lounge room when port, liqueurs or cognac would be offered.

If you are serving a buffet meal:

- have plenty of comfortable seats
- cover the serving table with a tablecloth and decorate with flowers, fruit, balloons or ornaments
- arrange plates, cutlery and napkins together
- avoid placing hot and cold foods side by side
- serve drinks from a separate table or bar
- use oil or gas burners under hot dishes
- have an area where guests can place used plates and glasses when they have finished their meal.

Table conversation and how to make it happen

To make sure everyone is involved in conversation spend time thinking about who your guests are: What do they do? Have they travelled? Are they talkers or listeners? Do they share the same interests? No matter how informal the occasion, success depends on how your guests mingle. If you spot a lull in the conversation, ask a question and start the ball rolling again.

Remember that other guests may be as shy as you are and unsure of how to start a conversation, so even a question like: 'How did you meet [name of hosts]?' will get you started. Make sure you speak to guests on other side of you and, if possible, the person sitting opposite you. Watch for anyone who seems to be 'out of' the conversation and draw them in by saying, 'I was just saying to John that this election should be an interesting one' so they know what you were talking about and can join in at that point.

One of the benefits of moving away from the dinner table to have coffee in the lounge room or out on the patio is that it enables guests to smoke and provides the opportunity to chat with those guests they haven't spoken with before.

SOME 'DON'TS' OF TABLE CONVERSATION

- Don't swear.
- Don't tell long-winded stories.
- Don't talk over people; in fact, avoid talking loudly at all.
- Don't interrupt when someone is speaking.
- Don't speak in another language.
- Don't laugh uproariously and slap other diners on the back.
- Don't gossip about or denigrate absent mutual friends or associates.
- Don't dominate the conversation by talking about a subject or a person that others don't know.
- Don't talk constantly about yourself, how you feel, and what you think.
- Don't answer any question with just 'yes' or 'no' because this makes it extremely difficult for the other person to maintain a conversation with you.
- Don't talk about your ex-spouse.
- Don't talk about your diet—guests don't want to know what gluten does to your intestines.
- Don't talk about your ex mother-in-law and how she broke up your marriage or drove your father-in-law to drink.

Smoking

If someone lights up in your home or car and you're averse to this practice, say 'I'm sorry, we don't smoke in the house/car'. It's illegal to smoke in any communal office or public space. It is impolite if you're a reformed smoker or a non-smoker to comment on other people's personal habits.

Drinking to excess

Drinking to excess is unwise under any circumstances. As a host, you have a responsibility to your guests not to suggest 'one for the road' and not to allow anyone to drive if they're over the legal alcohol limit. As a guest it's poor etiquette to get your gear off or hit on your host's partner. Drink loosens the tongue, so if you offend anyone apologise immediately and go home. The next day you should either ring and apologise again, or send a note and flowers.

Butter-fingers

Even if you weren't drunk but you broke a crystal wineglass or spilt red wine on the carpet, apologise and offer to replace the glass or pay for the carpet cleaning. If either of these situations apply, send flowers and a note the next day repeating your apology.

Chapter 4
EATING OUT AND
FINE DINING

More and more people these days spend a large amount of their disposable incomes on restaurant dining. And why not, with the quality of food in today's restaurants being second to none and our busy lifestyles often leaving people with no time to prepare their own meals. Fine dining gives the flexibility of eating well and having extra time to do the things we like to do.

If you have friends who love to eat out and invariably kick off the evening with a dozen caviar oysters, then munch their way through huge portions of prime fillet polished off with crêpes suzettes and washed down with the finest red, while you nibble on pasta and a green salad (and drink only one glass of the finest red) and then you all split the bill 50/50, you need to change your *modus operandi* (or your friends). You should either go to ethnic restaurants that are BYO or where the buffet is a set price, or to restaurants where the menu offers a set price, for example, three courses for $40.00. When you eat with friends who choose roughly the same priced meals as you do, then by all means, split the bill down the middle after adding the tip of approximately ten per cent—only if you've been happy with the service, of course.

TABLE ETIQUETTE

As Oscar Wilde once said: 'The world was my oyster but I used the wrong fork.' When you sit down at the table, the easiest way to remember which knife, fork and spoon to use is to start at the outside on the left, and the outside on the right and work your way inwards. The same applies to the glassware—there may be several glasses for sherry or champagne, wine and water but take the glass on the right and work in to the left.

Food is also served from the left and empty plates are removed from the right. Serving platters are offered from the left.

How to hold your cutlery
The fork
Hold your fork in your left hand by the handle; not too close to the prongs (or tines). Use your index finger to balance your fork by running it down the handle and push *small* portions of the food onto the top of the fork with your prongs facing downwards, then place it this same way (prongs facing down) in your mouth.

The *only* time that your fork may be held in your *right hand* and turned upside down and used as a 'shovel' is if you are eating a 'fork dish' such as curry with rice, risotto or pasta.

The knife
Hold the knife with the handle toward the centre of the palm so that your fingers are not touching the food. Spear meat with the fork and cut it off with the knife, but cut only one piece at a time.

The fish fork
Fish forks are easy to recognise because of their unusual shape. They have slight indentations on the outermost tines for lifting the skeleton of the fish when it is served whole. Hold the fish fork in your left hand with the prongs down.

The fish knife
The fish knife does not have a sharp blade because fish is tender and requires little cutting. The fish knife is held like a fork (steadied between your index finger and middle finger and secured by your thumb).

The soup spoon
A soup spoon is held by the end of the handle with the first two fingers and balanced by the thumb. Soup is spooned away from you across the bowl and then the spoon is brought back over the bowl to your mouth so that any drips land in the bowl.

The dessert spoon
The desert spoon is held in the same way as a soup spoon but food is spooned from the bowl towards you.

Napkin usage

If the waiter does not lay it across your lap, do this yourself when you sit down. Never tuck it into your collar or belt. When you've finished your meal, loosely fold your napkin and place it to the left of your place setting.

Finger bowls

If you order a food that is particularly messy or difficult to eat, you'll find that you're usually provided with a finger bowl—a small glass bowl with warm water and either a slice of lemon or rose petals floating in it. Dip your fingers into the bowl and then wipe them on your napkin; your waiter will remove the finger bowl when you've finished.

Cutlery savvy for tricky foods

Just as we think we've got a handle on table manners, we can be confronted with something as daunting as a whole artichoke or a plate of pasta, which can be awkward to eat. The good news is that you don't need cutlery for the artichoke because you can eat it with your fingers; the bad news is that you could finish up wearing most of your pasta if you don't keep your fork firmly on the plate when winding it up. Below is a list of the cutlery commonly used for tricky foods:

- oysters—usually served with the appropriate utensils on the same plate
- pâté can be spread onto crackers with the spreader provided
- fish—if you order fish as a main, a waiter will replace your cutlery with a fish knife and fork
- sorbet, which is like an iced dessert, can be savoury or fruit flavoured and is served to cleanse the palate before the next course. It comes with its own spoon on the underplate
- salad can be served *before*, *during* or *after* the main course and a small salad plate or bowl may be provided for it together with a salad knife and fork at your place setting
- dessert forks and spoons may be placed above your plate or in your cutlery line-up or brought out when you order dessert
- cheese can be served either before or after dessert. At a very formal banquet, separate cutlery would usually be provided.

WHAT TO DO WHEN YOU SIT DOWN

Don't start eating in case you have to say grace or toast the queen or country. When your host has started on their bread roll you can too. Never cut your bread roll with your knife; tear off a bite-sized piece, butter it and eat. The remainder of the bread roll should still be intact. All spreads should be put on the side of your bread and butter plate and added to the individual mouthful of bread just before you eat it.

It's polite to wait until each guest has received their meal, although if your host or other diners tell you to begin eating, do so.

Only salt from a salt mill or pepper from a pepper mill are ground directly over your meal; if salt comes in a small dish with a tiny spoon, carefully spoon the salt you require onto the right-hand side of your plate and sprinkle it with your fingers as required. Always taste your meal first before adding condiments.

If the food doesn't arrive all at once ...

If the meal is coming, the waiter will inform the host of how long it's likely to be and they can decide whether to encourage guests to start eating or to wait a few minutes. Likewise, if the host or a guest sends their dish back, the host should request that other guests begin eating.

If you drop your cutlery

Don't pick up the dropped cutlery and place it back on the table or, even worse, continue to use it. If you inform the waiter, he will retrieve the cutlery and replace it for you. If your cutlery or crockery is unclean, discreetly inform the waiter who will replace it. The same applies if you spot a foreign object in your meal—quietly signal the waiter who will replace the meal.

How to handle dietary restrictions

If you have dietary restrictions, you should have warned the person organising the function when you accepted their invitation that there are certain things that you cannot eat. Nevertheless, if this warning has been forgotten or overlooked and you're confronted with something you can't eat, tell your host as quietly as possible. They will try to provide you with something else, but if this can't be done, assure the waiter and other guests that you're happy to skip that course. However, if it is an accompaniment, such as mushrooms or broccoli, it's acceptable to leave it on the plate.

If you have food in between your teeth

Ask the waiter for a toothpick, cover your mouth and use the tooth-pick in your right hand to remove the morsel. The same technique is used if the food is inedible or 'off'—take it out of your mouth unobtrusively and leave it on the side of your plate.

Watching the speed at which you eat

Don't guzzle your food, but don't dawdle either. Keep an eye on the speed at which others are eating so that you don't race ahead and be the first to finish, or are too slow so that others have to sit and cool their heels while you finish each course (especially if you've been talking too much!).

When to thank waiters and hospitality staff

Although you should show gratitude to the wait staff when you're eating out, thanking them excessively is disruptive to your table con-versation and should be avoided. A good rule is to thank the waiter when they refill your wineglass, bring you another drink, bring your meal to the table, or serve vegetables or accompaniments directly onto your plate.

What to do at the end of the meal

When you've finished eating, put your knife and fork together vertically on the plate with the prongs of the fork pointing upwards and the blade of the knife facing in. They should be touching and running from north to south down the plate.

The waiter may bring damp, steamed towels which are used to wipe your hands and mouth only. Leave the towel on the left of your plate on top of your napkin until it's removed by the waiter.

If the meal is a special occasion and you would like to pay for the wine (and have been the one to order it), place your credit card near your place setting to serve as a signal.

If your group intends to split the bill, this should have been arranged earlier with one person nominated to pay and be reimbursed. Avoid quibbling over who ate what; divide the bill evenly unless you only had an entrée and soft drink and others had a three-course meal, beer and wine.

When you rise to leave, escort your guests outside to say goodbye. If one of your guests needs a taxi, ask the waiter or the receptionist to organise booking a taxi for them and then wait for the taxi to arrive before you leave.

If you were a guest, sending a 'thank you' note to the host would be a lovely idea and would certainly be appreciated.

What to do if you have to leave the table

If you must leave the table for any reason, fold your napkin and leave it on the left near your side plate.

When you leave the table, cross the knife and fork across your plate with the sharp side of the knife facing inwards and the prongs or tines of the fork facing downwards. A well-trained waiter will not remove your plate if you leave it with the knife and fork crossed as described above. Unfortunately, not all restaurant professionals are well trained, so if one attempts to take your plate while you are still eating, just politely say, 'I'm sorry, I haven't finished yet'.

FOURTEEN DINING 'DON'TS'

1. Don't tuck your napkin into the neckline of your dress, shirt or belt.
2. Don't put your knife in your mouth—or lick it.
3. Don't overload your plate if it's a buffet meal.
4. Don't slather your food with salt and pepper before tasting it.
5. Don't chew with your mouth open.
6. Don't put your handbag, briefcase, glasses, keys, pager or mobile phone on the table.
7. Don't lean across the table or another person to reach something—ask for it to be passed.

---

8. Don't push your plate or placemat away from you when you finish eating.
9. Don't turn your fork upside down and use it as a shovel.
10. Don't do any grooming at the table, other than lipstick.
11. Don't sit with your elbows on the table holding your knife and fork so that they are pointing upwards.
12. Don't wave your knife and fork around in the air to make a point when you are talking.
13. Don't put your bread roll in the gravy or sauce to 'mop up'.
14. Don't gnaw bones—you can pick up smaller bones in your left hand and daintily nibble at them.

How to handle tricky foods

The easiest way to handle tricky foods like crab or corn is to not order them! However, if you lust after lamb chops it's a pity to avoid them just because they require a little dexterity. Here are the tricks and tips to eating tricky foods.

Artichokes

Artichokes can be served either hot with melted butter, or cold with vinaigrette. If a side plate isn't offered, place the used leaves on the side of your plate. If a small bowl of melted butter is served, dip the leaf into the butter before eating it. When you've finished the leaves, scrape off the rest of the fronds and eat the heart with a knife and fork.

Asparagus

If the asparagus is served as a vegetable with a meal, it's eaten with a knife and fork. If, however, it is served as an appetiser with sauce on the tips, pick up the spear in your fingers, dip the tip in the sauce and then bite it off.

Avocado

An avocado served in its shell is eaten with a spoon and will usually come with salad dressing, or even seafood, in the cavity. If the avocado is sliced on the plate or in a salad, simply eat it with a fork.

Balmain (Moreton Bay) bugs

The best part of a 'bug' is the fleshy meat in the tail. Use a seafood pick—a long thin implement with a pointy, two-pronged tip—to delve into the shell and pry the flesh out. If no pick is provided, use your fingers and ask for a fingerbowl or a paper napkin.

Bread and butter

If butter pats or curls are used, pick up one with the spreader or small fork provided and place it on the edge of your bread and butter plate. Once you have eaten that piece of butter on your slice of bread or bread roll, break off another piece of bread, take another piece of butter and repeat the process.

Caviar and its accompaniments

If caviar is passed to you in a bowl with its own spoon, put a small teaspoonful onto your plate, then use the individual serving spoons in each bowl to take small amounts of minced onion, sieved egg whites and yolks, as well as a few lemon slices and a couple of toast quarters. Put the caviar and the accompaniments onto the toast and eat it using your fingers.

If you're at a cocktail party or reception where prepared caviar canapés are being passed on trays, simply lift one off the plate and pop it into your mouth.

Cheese

As an hors d'oeuvre, cheese is spread on a cracker or bread using a cheese knife. However, when cheese is served with a salad, you spread it on a cracker or a small piece of bread with either a fork or knife, or else a piece of cheese may be broken off on your plate with a fork and eaten with lettuce.

Soft, runny cheeses, such as brie and camembert, are always spread with a cheese knife, salad knife or butter knife.

Dessert cheeses are usually served with fruit and are easily handled. Quarter, core or pare the apples or ripe pears and eat the cheese with a fork and the fruit with either a fork or your fingers.

Cheese should be served at room temperature.

Clams and mussels

Lift both halves of the shell (if the shell doesn't open during steaming, don't eat the contents!), and then separate by pulling out the neck, dip first into a cup of broth and then into melted butter and eat in one bite.

Corn

There are two methods of eating corn on the cob. The first is to hold the corncob at each end using the small tongs provided and bite into it; the second method is to hold the corncob in your left hand by the prong provided and cut from top to bottom, slicing the kernels onto the plate.

Crab

If the crab is served whole, break one leg from the body and crack it into sections with a nutcracker. Remove the delicate crabmeat with a fork or seafood pick and then dip it into melted butter or sauce.

Dessert

Dessert can be eaten with the fork in the left hand with the prongs down, and the spoon in the right hand. You eat the dessert with the spoon and use the fork as a 'pusher' or to secure certain desserts (such as tarts). It's acceptable to swap hands and use the fork on its own, but you should never eat with just the spoon and ignore the fork—unless you're eating ice cream, mousse or pudding.

Figs

Fresh figs served as an appetiser with prosciutto are eaten skin and all with a knife and fork. If the little stem is still on the fig, cut it off.

If the figs are served as a dessert—quartered and drenched in orange juice or cream—they're eaten with a fork and spoon.

Fish

To eat fish with a fish knife and fork, hold the fish fork in your left hand with the prongs down. The fish knife is held like a fork. Use the fish knife to cut the fish and guide it onto the back of your fork.

French onion soup

Unlike other soups that you come across, French onion soup is served with a slice of French bread covered with cheese. To avoid the cheese forming a 'sticky bridge' between your bowl and your mouth, twirl a small amount of cheese onto your spoon and press the spoon edge against the side of your bowl to sever the thread of cheese.

Lobster

Usually, a lobster will be served to you in halves; if it isn't, you may prefer to ask the waiter to have it cut in the kitchen. Dip the meat in butter, mayonnaise or the side sauce, pull off the small claws, sucking (quietly) on the ends as if you were drinking through a straw. When eating lobster, you may need to wear a bib (and it's a good idea to). If a bib isn't provided, this is the only time it's acceptable to tuck a napkin into your collar.

Oysters (fresh)

For fresh oysters served in the half-shell, use an oyster fork. Hold the shell with your left hand and remove the oyster whole with the fork in your right hand. Dip the oyster in the sauce and eat it in one mouthful. It is acceptable in the case of Oysters Kilpatrick, which has a delicious sauce, to lift the oyster shell in the left hand and empty the remaining sauce straight into your mouth.

Pasta

To eat long pasta such as fettuccine or spaghetti, a fork should be held in the right hand and three to five strands of pasta twisted, low on the plate, into a circle around the fork. Sometimes a large spoon is provided, in which case keep the spoon *on the plate* and twist the pasta around the fork in your left hand on top of the upturned spoon, which is held in your right hand. *Never* cut long pasta.

Pâté

Pâté may be served either before dinner or with the salad during a meal. If it's served to you with cocktails, spread it thickly on crackers or small pieces of toast and eat it with your fingers. If pâté accompanies the salad course, it may be passed around in a ring mould; in that case, lift off a slice or serve a spoonful onto your plate along with a cracker or slice of toast and prepare a small open sandwich.

Peas

Squash peas with mashed potato or parsnip mash onto the back of your down-turned fork. If the meal is informal and the dish served is something like curry with rice and peas, then it's acceptable to take the fork in your right hand and turn it up the other way.

Prawns

Cocktail prawns are eaten with a fork, whereas large prawns are eaten in two bites and shrimp fried Oriental-style can be lifted up with your fingers by the tail and dipped into the serving sauce.

If the prawn is whole and unpeeled, pull off the head, lift the shell and legs away from the body and pull off the tail.

Salad

Salad can be served either before, with or after the main course and a small plate or individual salad bowl is usually placed at the top left-hand side of your table setting. If you eat the salad at the same time as your main course, you will use the same knife and fork as you use for the main course. Don't put the salad on your main meal plate, however; place it on the salad plate or bowl provided.

Snails

Hold the pair of tongs provided with your left hand and grip the snail shell. With your right hand, pry out the snail with the two-pronged fork provided.

Sorbet

Sorbet—an ice treat made from fruit juice, egg whites and milk—is eaten directly from the glass or dish; when you've finished, leave the spoon on the underlying plate.

Soup

Soup should be spooned away from you, angling the bowl away from you. Sip gently from the side of the spoon nearest to you, don't put the whole soup spoon in your mouth. When you're finished, put the upturned spoon on the right-hand side of the bowl on top of the underplate.

Common foreign terms found on menus

Here is a quick guide to the most common foreign terms found on menus (approximate phonetic pronunciation given):

Aglio (al-yo): Italian for 'garlic', so if dish is described as *con aglio* it means 'with garlic'.

Agnello (an-yellow): Italian for 'lamb'.

Al forno (al-four-no): Means anything baked or roasted in an Italian restaurant.

Antipasto (an-tee-pas-tow): The Italian equivalent of French hors d'oeuvres, which are small offerings served with drinks before a meal.

Au gratin (oh grar-tarn): A French crust made from breadcrumbs mixed with cheese.

Béarnaise (bay-ar-nays): A French sauce made of egg yolks, butter, tarragon vinegar and herbs; usually served over beef.

Béchamel (besh-a-mel): A French white sauce served as the basis for a mornay sauce, such as that used in lobster mornay, or the sauce used between sheets of pasta in lasagne.

Beurre (burr): French for 'butter', so if the dish is described as *avec buerre* it means 'with butter'.

Bisque (bisk): A French thick shellfish soup, such as Lobster Bisque.

Boeuf (berf): French for 'beef'.

Bouché (boo-shay): French for a very small vol au vent (vole-oh-von); served as an appetiser.

Bouillabaisse (boo-ya-base): French thick soup or stew of fish and shellfish, flavoured with tomatoes, garlic and herbs.

Brochette (bro-shet): French for beef, chicken or fish served on a skewer.

Bruschetta (brew-shetta): Toasted Italian bread with a topping of fresh tomatoes and basil or *tapenade* (a paste, for instance, of black olives with anchovies and basil).

Cacciatora (catchy-a-tora): An Italian sauce of tomatoes, onions, capsicum, wine and olives, for instance, Chicken Cacciatora.

Cannelloni (can-e-low-nee): Italian tubes of pasta filled with meat, chicken or vegetarian stuffing.

Carbonara (car-bo-nar-a): A rich Italian sauce of smoked ham or bacon, cheese, cream and eggs which is served over pasta.

Carpaccio (car-par-chee-o): Paper-thin Italian slices of raw meat. Usually served cold.

Cassata (cass-art-a): In Italian means a combination of three ice creams—chocolate, strawberry and pistachio—with meringue and cream filling and served with glazed fruits.

Cervelles (cher-vell): French for 'brains' or, in Italian, *cervelli* (cher-velly).

Champignons (shom-pin-nons): French for mushrooms or, in Italian, *fungi* (foon-gee).

Citron (sit-ron): French for 'lemon'.

Consommé (con-somay): A French thin, broth-like soup.

Coquilles (cock-eey): French for 'scallops'.

Crêpe (kray-p): A thin French form of pancake.

Crevettes (krev-ette): French for 'prawns'; in Italian *gamberi* or *scampi*, which are usually fried.

Croutons (crew-ton): French for small pieces of fried bread usually served with soup.

Dolci (doll-chee): Italian for sweets of any kind.

Dolmades (doll-mar-theez): Greek stuffed vine leaves.

Escargot (es-car-go): French for 'snails'.

Fagioli (fage-ee-o-lee): Italian for 'dried beans'.

Flambé (flom-bay): French for 'flamed', as in a dish being 'flamed' at your table, e.g Strawberries Flambé.

Flat Italian pasta or *fettuccine verdi* (vair-dee): green pasta.

Formaggio (for-marj-ee-oh): Italian for 'cheese'.

Freddo (fray-do): Italian for 'cold'.

Frutta di mare (froota dee mar-e): Italian for 'fruit of the sea' or mixed seafood.

Gateau (gat-oh): French for 'cake'.

Gelato (jell-ah-toe): Italian ice cream.

Gnocchi (noc-ee): Italian dish of dumplings made of ground potatoes, semolina or polenta, usually served with a creamy sauce.

Hollandaise (holl-on-days): A French cream sauce made with butter and egg yolks.

Huitre (wee-tr): French for 'oyster'.

Insalata (in-sal-arta): Italian for 'salad'.

Kebab (ke-babb): Turkish cooked meat on a stick.

Lapin (lap-arn): French for 'rabbit'.

Marinara (mar-in-ar-a): Italian for a tomato concasse with seafood; served over pasta.

Mezze plate (mettze): A range of Turkish style dips and breads served as an appetiser.

Minestrone (min-e-stroe-nay): An Italian, thick and hearty tomato-based vegetable soup with noodles.

Moules (mule): French for 'mussels' or, in Italian, *cozze* (cottze).

Mousse (moose): A very light French form of frothy mixture eaten sweet or savoury.

Mozzarella (mot-zar-ella): A semi-firm Italian cheese used in baking pasta.

Nachos (natch-ohs): A Mexican dish of corn chips served with chicken or beef, beans, cheese, chilli and guacamole.

Oeuf (erf): French for 'egg'; *uovo* (oo-oh-vo) in Italian

Papillotes (pap-ee-yot): In French means 'buttered paper'; when used on menus it refers to that in which the food is cooked.

Parmigiano (par-midge-ee-an-o): Italian Parmesan cheese, hence Veal Parmigiano is veal with melted cheese, shaved ham and chopped basil.

Pasta: A generic name for all kinds of European noodles.

Paupiettes (po-pee-yet): French stuffed rolls of meat.

Pesce (pess-ke): Italian for 'fish'; *psari* (pss-ar-ee) in Greek.

Petits fours (petty four): Dainty French cakes, usually bite-sized, which are often beautifully decorated and served with after-dinner coffee.

Poire (pwar): French for 'pear'.

Poisson (pwa-sson): French for 'fish'.

Polenta (poll-ent-a): Italian ground-up corn meal.

Pollo (poll-oh): Italian for chicken; *kotopoulo* (coto-pullo) in Greek.

Pomme (pom): French for 'potato'; *patata* in Greek.

Potage (pot-arge): French for 'soup'.

Poulet (poo-leh): French for 'chicken'.

Praline (prah-lin): A French type of burnt, thin, almond toffee, which is usually served with coffee.

Prosciutto (prosh-yoo-toe): Italian ham.

Quenelles (ken-elle): A French rissole made of chicken or fish, often served with sauce.

Ragoût (ra-goo): A French stew.

Ratatouille (rat-a-too-ee): French vegetable stew or casserole.

Riz (ree): French for 'rice'.

Sacher torte (sakka taut-eh): A very rich Austrian chocolate cake named after the Sacher Hotel in Vienna.

Sashimi (sash-ee-me): Japanese raw fish.

Savoiardi (sav-oy-ardi): An Italian pale, dry finger biscuit which is often served with desserts such as ice cream or zabaglione.

Scallopini (scall-op-een-ee): In Italian are thin, flattened slices of veal fillet, as in Veal Scallopini.

Saltimbocca (sol-tim-bocka): literally, 'jump in the mouth', an odd Italian name for bundles of veal, ham and sage cooked in wine and then lightly fried.

Sorbet (saw-bay): A French frozen, flavoured, sweet or savoury ice which is served either between courses to freshen the palate or as a finish to a heavy meal.

Tagliatelle (tal-ya-telly): An Italian flat noodle.

Tapas (ta-pas): Appetisers popular throughout Spain.

Terrine (ter-een): A kind of very coarse French pâté served with toast or potted meat in a mould.

Tiramisu (tirra-miss-u): Italian cake-style dessert soaked in brandy.

Torte (taut-eh): German name for an elaborate cake or tart.

Tortellini (tort-elle-eeny): These are small 'pockets' of Italian pasta stuffed with a meat or savoury filling and served with a sauce of some kind.

Tournedos (torn-ay-dough): French for a small fillet of beef, usually served grilled or sautéed.

Turkish delight: A gelatine-based Turkish sweet dusted with fine icing sugar.

Vichyssoise (vee-shee-swahz): French for potato and leek soup, usually served cold.

Vinaigrette (vin-eh-grett): French for oil and vinegar dressing.

Vitello (vitt-ell-oh): Italian for 'veal'.

Vol au vent (voll-oh-von): French puff pastry case, which can have a sweet (custard) or savoury filling (tuna in white sauce). The latter is often served as an hors d'oeuvre (or-derv) with drinks before a meal or, if larger, can be an entrée.

Zabaglione (za-bah-lee-oh-ne): A delicious, light Italian dessert made from frothy eggs mixed with marsala (a dark sweet wine) and sugar, and beaten over a 'water bath' to a ribbon-like consistency.

WINE AND DRINKS

Serving the right wine with food ensures a meal is enjoyed at its best. A general guideline suggests that white wine complements fish, poultry or veal while red wine seems to go better with lamb and beef, but it is often the way in which food is cooked and the ingredients used which influence the flavour and therefore determine which wine best complements the completed dish. Delicate flavours should balance delicate ingredients, and powerful flavours should balance powerful ingredients.

White wines
Riesling

A young riesling is an excellent accompaniment to spicy salads or Asian foods and its crisp flavour makes it a good summer wine. An aged riesling (say over fourteen years old) would be ideal with a richer dish, such as marinated quail, as it's able to stand up against chilli and garlic, which are the enemies of many wines. It is also the perfect dessert wine and is gaining popularity these days as an accompaniment to cheese.

Sauvignon blanc

Sauvignon blanc is particularly good with smoked salmon and delicate seafood, like grilled scallops or whiting.

Semillon

A Hunter Valley semillon is very delicate with an alcoholic content of between 10–12 per cent and is delicious with seafood. On the other hand, most of the South Australian semillons are more robust and usually quite oaky; this makes them ideal with creamy sauces, chicken or pasta.

Verdelho

Verdelho goes well with anything that has a robust flavour, such as focaccia with salami, feta cheese and black olives.

Chardonnay

Chardonnay can be wooded or unwooded, and light through to fruity. An older chardonnay would complement pasta with creamy sauces and rich seafoods, like lobster, mud crab or bisque, while a young, crisp chardonnay would go well with lightly pan-fried fish.

Red wines
Cabernet sauvignon

While a young, robust cabernet sauvignon with lots of tannin would be excellent with pork, a more mature, mellow cabernet sauvignon with more earthy characteristics would be superb with lamb or beef.

Merlot

This wine is an interesting 'bridge' between cabernet sauvignon and shiraz in that it's usually only medium-bodied and is softer, with less tannin. It is an excellent accompaniment for chicken or rabbit.

Grenache

Grenache is bright in colour with a vibrant, fruity aroma.

Pinot noir

This wine has a high alcohol content of between 13–15 per cent and is ideal with a barbecued steak; however it's probably not an ideal wine to drink at lunch if you're intending to return to work in the afternoon.

Shiraz

Shiraz is a versatile, full-bodied wine with plenty of tannin, so it goes well with beef or lamb. Because the flavour of shiraz ranges from the pepper and spice of grapes grown in colder growing areas to the fruitiness of grapes grown in warmer climes, it's a wine which is best drunk with a simple meal (like steak), where the juice of the meat will soften the tannin of the wine. It's also a good accompaniment to rich savoury stews like bouillabaisse.

Champagne/sparkling wines

Unless a wine actually comes from the Champagne region in France, it shouldn't be referred to as 'champagne' but rather as 'sparkling wine', however, you'll find that colloquially it's often called 'champagne' or 'bubbly'. Because of its high acidity, nothing beats serving sparkling wine as an aperitif.

Grilled salmon, tuna steaks or seafood terrine are perfect with sparkling wine, as is a Roquefort soufflé, seafood risotto, fresh oysters, or an Italian-style antipasto platter as the saltiness of prosciutto, salami, olives and Parmesan cheese draws out the wine's flavour.

Always serve champagne and sparkling wine cold at about 6–8 degrees Celsius.

> If you're short of time, salt stirred into the ice and water in the ice bucket will drop the temperature and cut the chilling time in half.

ALL ABOUT WINE
Why do we taste the wine first?
To check the condition of the wine to see whether it is oxidised or 'corked'; not to ascertain whether or not you like it.

What is tannin?
Tannin (sometimes called 'grip') comes from the skin of the grapes and the wooden casks and tends to pucker up the inside of the cheeks in a similar way that black tea puckers the inside of the mouth.

What is meant by 'corked'?
'Corked' describes a wine affected by 'cork taint'—a dank, musty aroma found randomly in all brands of wine with natural corks.

If a wine has cork taint, it will smell like mouldy hessian or wet cardboard. If the wine has oxidised, it will be brown, flat, and smell and taste like sherry.

These problems most commonly apply to wine purchased by the glass, as the bottle may stand for two or three days and oxidisation can occur. If the wine is affected by cork taint you may send it back.

What is a sommelier?
A sommelier (se-mel-yer) is a wine waiter who orders wines, keeps the staff informed of what's in the cellar, suggests suitable wines to accompany the menu, and tastes the wines so that diners' questions can be answered by the staff. It's also the sommelier's role to teach the staff how to open and serve wine correctly.

HOW TO SERVE WINE
In a restaurant, the waiter will usually pour a little wine into the glass of the host, who will taste it and then ask the waiter to pour for the rest of the guests. Wine is both poured from the right and removed from the right.

If you're at dinner in someone's home, the host should taste the wine first and then serve the guests. When serving wine around the table, the women are usually served first, then the men, and finally the host's glass can be filled.

TEN TIPS ON SERVING, STORING AND ENJOYING WINE
(courtesy of Goundrey Fine Wines)

1. Ensure that the correct glass is used for the wine and check that glasses are clean, polished and unchipped.
2. Serve white wine and dessert wine at between 8–12 degrees Celsius. The lighter the style the cooler the end of the spectrum is suggested.
3. Some types of sherry, like Fino and Manzanilla, are improved with chilling and it's a good idea to put red wine in the refrigerator for thirty minutes or so prior to serving in summer.
4. Serve red wine, fortified wine, brandy and port at 'room temperature', i.e. between 18–22 degrees Celsius. It is preferable to think in terms of European room temperature. A light shiraz would be best served at 18 degrees and a fuller-bodied red wine, such as merlot, at 22 degrees Celsius.
5. Always check the wine before offering to guests in case it is oxidised or 'corked'. This can save considerable embarrassment, especially if you are trying to impress someone.
6. When pouring any wine, hold the bottle so that you swing the neck upwards and then twist the bottle slightly as you finish pouring so that it doesn't drip on the table, the placemat, or your guest!
7. Aged wines should be decanted prior to serving to allow them to 'breathe'. This can also dispel many unwanted characteristics or 'bottle stink'.
8. Never fill the glass to the brim, about two-thirds full allows you enough space to swirl the wine around and release the bouquet.
9. If your function is a 'come for drinks at 5.00 p.m.' allow about one hour per drink, although many will drink more quickly in the first hour and then slow down. Each 750ml bottle holds roughly six glasses.
10. Store wine with the bottle lying down in a cool dark place with minimal variation of temperature.

How to hold your wineglass

If it's a red wine served at room temperature, hold the glass at the *bottom of the bowl*. If it's white wine or champagne, which are served chilled, hold the glass *by the stem*, so that your body heat doesn't warm the wine.

How to hold a white wine glass

How to open champagne or sparkling wine bottles

If you're right-handed, place a napkin on top of your left arm and remove the foil cover from the neck of the bottle. There is no need to remove the wire casing that prevents the cork from turning into a dangerous projectile. Remove the little circular piece and then grasp the bottle by the base and give it six half turns anti-clockwise until you feel the cork beginning to loosen. Put the napkin over the cork and gently ease up the wire casing while pushing the cork upwards with your right thumb. If it won't dislodge, use either pliers or one of the commercial sparkling wine openers, which will have it out in a moment. If the cork does break, just pick out the pieces and pour—it won't affect the taste.

How to pour champagne

Tilt the glass on its side and pour the champagne in two movements so that the bubbles almost reach the brim of the glass. Then, when the frothing settles down, continue to fill the glass until it is two-thirds full. Don't lift the glass to the bottle; take the bottle to the glass.

Chapter 5

POLITE CONVERSATION AND CORRESPONDENCE

It can be awkward meeting strangers but this can be alleviated by asking 'open-ended' questions; that is, questions which can't be answered by 'yes' or 'no'. When the other person replies you should select part of the reply and develop it to continue the conversation. For instance, if someone has said that they enjoy travelling, tease them out by asking what it is they enjoy most—the people, the wine, the food, the culture and so on. Ask people about themselves—'Tell me, Rowena …' and listen to what Rowena says, pick out something interesting and say, 'How interesting. I had no idea …'

Rowena will be pleased that you find her interesting and will feel confident to go on talking. If you see someone who is 'out in the cold', look at them, smile, wait for Rowena to pause and include them in the conversation: 'Rowena is just telling me about …' Give other conversationalists your entire attention as there are few things more flattering to men and women than to feel people are interested in what they are saying.

Remember that listening is very important; look interested, don't interrupt, nod and perhaps say, 'I see' or 'Really?' to let the speaker know that you are interested in what they're saying.

HOW TO BE A CHAMPION CONVERSATIONALIST

There are some people that just about everyone loves to talk to because they're up-beat, positive and informative. Everyone wants to sit next to this person—the champion conversationalist. This person has mastered the art of conversation by:

• listening—the best asset of a good conversationalist is their ability to listen devotedly to what others are saying
• allowing every speaker to finish what they're saying
• being enthusiastic about other's stories and being visually alive through body language and expression

- smiling before saying something
- having a great sense of humour—the champion conversationalist can laugh at themselves without seeming negative
- charming even bored and belligerent guests
- filling in any conversational gaps or long silences
- talking about anything and everything—by being well-read with broad general knowledge
- steering a conversation towards new and interesting depths
- ignoring other's mistakes and not chastising or correcting them, especially when they make errors relating to grammar, pronunciation, or consistency of storyline
- looking people in the eye when talking to them
- knowing when it's a good time to talk business and when it's time to make small talk; offering opinions and ideas without being argumentative.

Some topics to get the ball rolling

Films, plays and musicals—these topics can lead to talk about actors, film gossip, the wizardry of special effects today, film locations—which leads you to talking about travel. You don't need to have travelled extensively to talk about exotic destinations. Watch documentaries and read the travel pages in the newspaper and travel magazines so you can nod intelligently when people talk about far-flung places they've visited. You just need to know where they're talking about to make the conversation work.

Music and musicals, study or educational courses, organisations, social clubs and charities, and art galleries and museums are also excellent topics of conversation. Reading not only broadens your mind, but also your conversation. Try to choose books that not only interest you, but lend themselves to discussion.

What you do for a living is usually a good topic unless you're an undertaker or in the secret service.

Restaurants are one of the best topics of conversation as people enjoy eating out, so swapping names and menus of good eateries is fun. This topic obviously leads in to wines which, again, can lead into wine tours, wine tastings, wine bargains and travel to wineries.

Pets can be an amusing source of discussion—just don't produce a photograph of your pet from your purse or wallet!

Whether it's canasta or cricket, cars or canoeing, discussing what you do as a hobby encourages your listener to tell you what they are interested in doing. Before you know it, you're immersed in an interesting conversation. And you thought you weren't a good conversationalist!

Dangerous ground

You can see that with so many topics to talk about, there's no need to gossip, name-drop or ridicule others. Personal remarks about other people should be limited to complimentary comments only and when relating a story, never use real names as you never know who knows who. If someone else starts to gossip, it's best to say if you know the person they're discussing, 'Joanne is a friend of mine, so I feel extremely uncomfortable talking about her like this' and if you don't know them, 'I don't know the person you're talking about but we shouldn't be discussing him/her when he/she isn't here to defend him/herself.' Having said that, if the gossip continues, excuse yourself and move away. Avoid repeating anything you do hear about a person. You don't know how true it is and how it can damage a person's reputation. Similarly, if friends or colleagues confide either personal or professional secrets to you, they've trusted you so don't disappoint them by repeating what they've told you.

If you're inclined to get excited during a conversation, remember not to interrupt when someone else is speaking, even if the story they're telling seems to be going nowhere. If they're very boring, excuse yourself and move to another group. You can always offer to top up their drink, or someone else's drink, or even your own drink, in order to move away from a conversation.

How to extinguish a conversational inferno

If a nasty row has erupted, stories are getting too ribald for mixed company, someone is telling sexist or racist jokes, or for any reason you feel that the conversation is out of control, say, 'I think we might move on from there, Jack' or 'I think we've heard enough about that for one night, Jack.' If Jack continues, a quiet word to his wife or partner about what a big day at work you have tomorrow will probably do the trick.

How not to be a bore

Keep your eyes peeled for telltale signs of boredom. Watch for body language and change the subject if you notice your discourse on quantum physics is producing glazed expressions in your listeners. If people begin to shuffle their feet, start to look around the room or at their watch, there's a good chance they're dying to make a fast getaway. Similarly, if they're slumping in their seat and haven't uttered a word in thirty minutes, they're bored. Just to help you here, the three most boring topics of conversation are diets, the family tree and personal health problems.

TELEPHONES, MOBILES AND EMAIL

Modern communication today involves the use of telephone, mobile phones and email to meet and greet friends, family, work colleagues and clients. It's important to be familiar with what is deemed appropriate when using these services.

Telephones

When answering the telephone you should always be welcoming and speak clearly. Never shout or speak too loudly into the mouth-piece. Say a simple 'hello' and either the phone number or your name when answering the telephone.

When leaving a message for someone, leave your full name and contact phone number, and always return calls promptly.

Mobile phones

When answering a mobile phone, the same etiquette applies as the telephone. You should always turn your mobile phone off in places where calls are not appreciated, such as at social gatherings, the cinema, lecture halls, the theatre, in church, in restaurants, in aeroplanes and, of course, at funerals!

If you're at a lunch or dinner with friends or colleagues but you have a sick child at home or are expecting an important message then explain the situation to them and apologise for the need to have your mobile on. Once you've taken the call or received the message turn off the phone.

Text messaging is also popular. Be sure that the text message is clear. Personal messages which may cause distress, such as cancelling a date, informing someone of a death, or ending a relationship, should never be in the form of a text message.

Emails

Email has tended to replace the written letter these days. When writing an email, be sure your message is clear—many misunderstandings do occur, especially with the use of capital letters, which can denote anger. Be brief and straight to the point, especially when sending business-related messages. But most importantly of all, do not send any material that is offensive in nature.

THANK YOUS, APOLOGIES AND WELL WISHES

When posting thank you notes, apologies or well wishes choose good quality, plain stationery with matching envelopes. Plain paper can be used for all your notes and won't date: white, cream or soft grey always look good but avoid paper that has flowers, hearts or cute animals on it.

If your budget allows you to have some stationery personalised, then do so. It should include your name, address and phone number.

Embossed ecru paper (the colour of unbleached linen) looks very elegant. If you feel you can't write enough to cover a whole page of note paper, you could have a card printed with your name, address and phone number across the top, which you can also use for invitations, thank you notes or enclosures. If you dislike writing notes, choose cards instead, where you only need to write six to eight lines. They should come with matching envelopes with your return address printed on them.

If you really want to make an impression, write in ink with a fountain or calligraphy pen. Never type the envelope of a personally handwritten letter and ensure your return address is on the flap of the envelope.

Different kinds of notes

Letters and cards will always begin with the word 'Dear' and end with either 'Yours sincerely' or, more informally, 'Fondest wishes'. If you don't know the person well, ring to ask how a difficult surname is spelt and to find out whether they like to be addressed as Ms or Mrs etc.

Thank you letters and notes

Letters and cards should be written promptly, be sincere and enthusiastic. If you are writing to thank for a gift of money or flowers, it's essential that you get your note away as soon as possible as the sender has no way of knowing you've received their gift until they hear from you. If you really find it difficult to write a letter, sending a pre-printed card is the solution since it is short.

Thank you cards for wedding gifts can match the design of the wedding invitation and need only be a couple of lines long. Try to mention the gift itself and how useful you think it is.

SAMPLE THANK YOU NOTE

Dear Joan and Bob,

Just a couple of lines to say how much Tim and I enjoyed our-selves last night.

We thought your daughter-in-law was a delightful girl and feel that she will settle well in Adelaide.

Joan, I would love the recipe for the mousse, Tim rarely eats dessert and he really loved it.

Once again thank you for including us in the family get-together.

Fondest regards,
Anna and Tim Priest

Notes of apology

If you find you have to cancel a date, it's important to let the host know as soon as possible. Ring (do not text message or email) to explain why you can't make it, and if it was an important get-together, such as a birthday, write a short note the next day saying you hope the party was a great success and repeat you were sorry not to be able to make it.

If you forget to go to someone's home for dinner, lunch or drinks, then you must apologise, no matter how difficult you find it, by a note or flowers.

Notes of condolence

Don't undermine your friend's grief by trying to be too positive (unless the deceased suffered through a long illness). Keep your note honest, brief and sombre—as befitting the occasion. Assure your friend you don't expect them to reply but let them know you are anxious to be supportive in any way.

If, on the other hand, you're the bereaved party and the one receiving letters of condolence, keep a list of those kind enough to contact you and at a time when you feel you can, try to reply. If you feel unable to reply, then a card with a message of thanks should be sent.

Letters of congratulations

When a friend wins a golf tournament, is promoted at work, announces his or her engagement, has his or her first child or wins an award, write a short note to them saying how pleased you are for him or her. Since so few people write notes these days, it will be well received.

Christmas cards

Christmas time is a perfect opportunity to keep in touch with people you rarely see throughout the year. If you do have cards printed, it's still nice to add a couple of personal, handwritten lines and to address envelopes by hand.

If you choose to have a personalised Christmas card, you may decide against a religious one and choose something neutral or with an Australian theme. Make sure you have your name and address on the flap of the envelope.

Chapter 6

FORMALS, DATING AND LIVING TOGETHER

Everyone likes to be in a warm and intimate relationship, sharing experiences and interests with the perfect mate. Relationships come in different ways throughout life and knowing the appropriate etiquette can keep them alive and enjoyable

THE SCHOOL FORMAL

This tradition is usually at the end of years 10 and 12. Many years ago, the end-of-school dance was a very simple affair where the only costs involved were a dress and a corsage for the girl and the hire of a dinner suit for the young man. Today's formal is a very different story as girls and boys are chic, elegant and often avant-garde. For many teenagers, the school formal is more than a party to mark the end of their school days, it's the beginning of their life as an adult, so their dress and behaviour reflects this attitude.

Some parents are prepared to pay thousands of dollars to ensure that their offspring can leave school 'in style', but such extravagance is unnecessary. A good time can be had if parents set financial and behavioural guidelines.

Most attend their formal with their circle of friends, or as a couple in groups. Either sex can ask a date for the event. Many partygoers congregate at one student's home for drinks beforehand, which provides an excellent opportunity for a photograph of the host parents with their child and their child's date, and also for a photo of the group. A professional photograph or video can be a good investment as it provides an excellent memento of the occasion and the cost can be shared. You should ask the ball organisers if they have any objection to a family member or a professional photographer taking a video of the proceedings.

Limousines are an excellent idea as no one is responsible for transport and the costs can be shared.

Fashion for girls

First of all is the dress. Fashion dictates that black is always a very popular choice, but dresses should not be too low cut. Whatever shoes you choose, make sure that they're comfortable for dancing. Many girls like to have their existing shoes dyed to match their dress; otherwise strappy, high-heeled sandals are popular. Bags are often made of fabric to match the dress, although beaded bags are also very popular accessories.

Many hair salons today offer school formal packages for hair, make-up, and a pedicure and manicure. Headpieces made of flowers are popular and hair stylists can design a style to complement the headpiece.

Corsages can be worn on the dress, wrist, handbag or high on the upper arm.

Fashion for boys

Outfits are varied. Blue suits, red suits, 'Liberace' jackets, gangster suits complete with black shirts and hats and white ties with matching silk scarves, suits worn with long dark ties instead of bow ties— all are available for hire. Many young couples like to wear matching outfits, for instance, something with a *Great Gatsby* theme.

Just make sure the shoes are comfortable and go easy on the black polish as it comes off on your partner's shoes if you have more than one left foot.

These days the short back and sides is dead. Boys can be as adventurous as they like to be, and hats that complement their outfit are popular.

Some boys may opt to wear buttonholes, usually in the same colour as their partner's corsage.

Partying on after the formal

Many groups like to party on and hire private adjoining rooms or suites at top city hotels. In some cases, elaborate breakfasts can be arranged, either at the hotel, a popular beach, or a fun place like McDonald's. Parents should set guidelines so that they know what is happening, where it's happening, and who will be there.

DATING

Apart from the usual meeting through work, friends or family, few people enjoy 'cruising' clubs, pubs and bars. However, the gym is a good place to meet, as is going out with single men who are and always will be 'friends'—remember they have friends who may be interesting. Go with them when they meet their mates for drinks, football practice or weight lifting. One man leads to another. Don't hesitate to ask them if they know anyone they might think you would like; be frank about the fact that you're open to offers, and do the same with girlfriends. They may have single brothers, or an ex they think would be right for you. Rather than letting her set you up on a blind date, suggest casual drinks after work, or lunch with a group of friends. That way you can look him over without being obvious. If you like what you see, you can take it from there.

Today, dating services, meeting on the Internet, chat lines and electronic advertisements in which you leave a pre-taped message in a voicemail box number are also popular. Don't give your full name or address and make sure your first date is in a public place and that you let a friend know where you're going and who you're meeting.

Can you ask a man out on a date?

Of course you can! If you meet someone you think has potential, mention in passing that you have a couple of tickets to a concert and whether he would like to join you (he can only say 'no'). Or ask him to go to a friend's barbecue with you next weekend (and then get her to organise one!). If your office has drinks after work every Friday night, invite him to come along. Make the invitation casual so he doesn't feel obliged to attend if he doesn't want to, or if he's not free.

Asking a man out on a date requires subtlety. You need to get the body language into gear—send out some signals, smile, look interested when he's speaking, laugh, mention casually that you love Indian food (if that doesn't work mention that a few of you are going for Indian food tomorrow night) and if he picks up the signals he might suggest you both go out the following night.

Is it OK to ring someone you've just met?

If you meet someone at a party or bar and you think he or she is interesting, it's better if you know someone who knows him or her to make the call to set up a casual meeting. If you don't, it's probably safer to text or email the person with a casual suggestion for a drink, coffee or film rather than to risk the embarrassment of a 'no' on the telephone.

If it's someone you've been out with a couple of times and you like them but they don't call you again, the same as above applies. If you feel you must ring, make it brief and light-hearted and if he or she doesn't ring you back, forget it. They are either not interested or in another relationship. But make sure you leave your number as perhaps he or she has lost it and that's why they haven't called.

Electroniquette

Email and text messaging are a safe and embarrassment-free way of making contact with someone you'd like to meet. If the person is not interested in you, then they just won't reply. If they want to let you down more easily, they can send you a brief but clear rejection which ends the courtship right there. On the positive side, you can flirt a little, and for people who are shy, this is a great way of getting a relationship off the ground. Avoid sending sexy messages as you don't know where they'll end up and don't give out personal details of your phone number or address, so if you do meet and the date is disastrous, ending the liaison at that point is simple. Keep the communication simple in the early stages and suggest group meetings if the person expresses some interest in you. If the person doesn't call, try once more in case they didn't get the message and then drop it. Either they are not interested or are already in another relationship.

How do you decline a date?

Get in early, drop a few hints around the office or during the conversation with the interested party about the fact that you're working at two jobs, studying for your MBA at night, and caring for an ailing aunt that lives with you. This should hopefully turn off any prospect of being asked out on a date. But if you still get asked out, thank him or her and tell them you have so little free time you spend it trying to catch up with family. The idea is to set the impression that there is no spot in our life for him or her so you don't hurt their feelings. None of us like to be rejected so declining a date should always be done with care and courtesy.

Going on blind dates

We've all been on disastrous dates, but blind dates can be very difficult indeed. Unfortunately, if you're shy or if you have persuasive friends, you may find yourself in the situation of having to go out with someone who you don't know from a bar of soap. The biggest problem most people face when it comes to blind dating is mastering the art of conversation. It can be nerve-racking—sometimes even more so if you find yourself actually liking the person you've been 'hooked up' with. However, blind dates (even ones where you don't meet Mr or Miss Right) can still be a lot of fun once you learn how to relax and guide the evening to a smooth anxiety-free conclusion.

NINE 'DOS' AND 'DON'TS' OF BLIND DATING

1. Do introduce yourself and tell your date who gave you their name and phone number.
2. Do meet your date at a public place and be on time.
3. Do tell a friend or family member where you're going and who you're going with.
4. Do split the bill so you don't feel under any obligation later in the evening.
5. Don't drink too much alcohol.
6. Don't accept a lift with your date; travel to the meeting place alone in your own car or in a taxi.
7. Don't go to a noisy bar where you can't hear each other talk.
8. Don't make the first date too long—take it slowly.
9. Don't invite your date back to your apartment and don't go to theirs if you're asked.

Going on first dates

Although with a first date you know the person you'll be spending the evening with, it can still be a daunting experience, so the time, place and ambience are critical factors. Many shy people make the mistake of choosing to see a movie or a play for a first date, which doesn't allow them the opportunity to chat with their date and find out who they are and what interests they have. If you do decide to see a movie or play, try to go for coffee afterwards, so that you'll have something to talk about.

Undoubtedly, the best place to take your first date is out for coffee, drinks, lunch or dinner. This way you will have plenty of time to get to know each other and if you're both shy or find you have nothing in common, at least you can talk about the food, the wine and the decor.

If it was your idea to go out, then it's up to you to choose the venue, although it would be polite to ask your date if they have any preferences. Think of what a failure your evening would be if you booked a lovely seafood restaurant only to find that your date was allergic to fish. You may like to offer your date a choice of two locations. Ideally, the restaurant you choose should be neither flashy nor cheap and nasty—middle of the range is best. Most importantly, the restaurant should have plenty of atmosphere, nice lighting, friendly and efficient waiters and good wine—all of which help to ease the often uncomfortable nature of first dates.

Dating manners

Who pays? If he's asked you out then he pays. If he takes you to dinner you could offer to buy the wine, pay for the taxi or for the parking. If you've asked him to a concert, he might offer to take you to dinner beforehand or to drinks or a nightclub afterwards. If it's a blind date, then split the bill down the middle (if you notice he divides the bill according to what he ate and what you ate, you might want to reconsider a second date!). If his mother brought him up to treat a woman like a lady, and unless you have a problem with that, let him pay. You can buy him a special gift as you get to know his tastes or invite him over for a home-cooked meal. Don't forget to either ring him the next day to thank him, or if you prefer, send an email. Texting runs a poor third as far as I'm concerned, but it's better than nothing.

If a man extends you little courtesies such as opening the car door for you or pulling out your chair, smile and thank him. He's been brought up well. If on the other hand he eats his peas off his knife, lets the door swing back in your face, or swears in front of your mother, maybe he isn't a long-term investment.

Unless you are both so inclined, a blind or first date shouldn't really finish up between the sheets (or anywhere else intimate for that matter). If it's been a great night and you're feeling very warm and fuzzy, a chaste kiss on the cheek really gives the message that you'd like to go on a date again.

If you change your mind about going on a date, or something comes up that you can't possibly cancel, let your date know as soon as possible. Never stand anyone up—it's not just discourteous, it's cruel. If on the other hand, your date is cancelling an outing with you, be sympathetic to the situation but don't suggest another date. Let them ring you again to organise another date; if they don't you'll know the cancellation was just an excuse.

Sexetiquette

Both men and women should be responsible about contraception and not assume that the other has taken precautions. Contraception is important not only to prevent pregnancy but is protection against sexually transmitted diseases (STDs) and women shouldn't feel embarrassed about refusing sex if the man is unwilling to 'don a condom'.

It's not good manners (nor is it kind) to criticise a lover's performance and even if he or she asks for a rating, don't be lulled into giving one. Similarly, don't compare past lovers and their techniques with the current model. And if you feel this partner is not right for you now and not likely to be in the future, breaking up should be done promptly before the other's feelings are further hurt.

TEN THINGS NOT TO TALK ABOUT ON A FIRST DATE

1. Your past partner or ex-wife and the reasons you broke up. Particularly avoid describing the details of court proceedings, the distress of the children, and how much you dislike their new partner.
2. Sex. This is the most intimate topic you can discuss and is too presumptuous for a 'getting to know you' first date.
3. Any illness, disease or aches and pains you might suffer from (avoid details of your last operation).
4. Any sport you're passionate about (unless you're both fans).
5. Your work (at least not continuously, and always modestly).
6. Money—what you earn, what your suit cost, your mortgage, your maintenance payments to a previous spouse.
7. Clothing or shopping (this topic will bore most men stiff!).
8. Your children and their day-to-day problems (or at least for not too long!).
9. Your pets and their little quirks.
10. Contentious issues such as race, religion or women's liberation.

TEN THINGS TO TALK ABOUT ON A FIRST DATE

1. Your hometown.
2. Food, restaurants and wine.
3. Travel.
4. Your favourite books, movies, plays and music.
5. Hobbies.
6. Ambitions and goals in life.
7. Your childhood (interesting anecdotes or happy memories only).
8. What a wonderful time you're having (a little flattery goes a long way!).
9. Politics. This subject is often thought to be taboo, but you may as well find out whether you are passionately opposed when it comes to politics—you will sooner or later.
10. Your date—find out about their childhood, work, family etc.

Faux pas and how to avoid them

While communication is vital for building intimacy in any relationship, there are some things best left unsaid:

You asked her what?

- Have you put on weight?
- Aren't you two married yet?
- Why don't you have children?
- Are you tired? You don't look well!
- How much did that cost?
- How old are you?
- When is the baby due? (or if she's pregnant, avoid saying, 'You look huge, when is the baby due?')
- Is that cellulite on your arms?
- Is that diamond real?
- Is that the best sex you've ever had?

You asked him what?

- Do you love me?
- Do I look fat in this dress?
- Is my cooking as good as your mother's?
- Can you see any cellulite on my legs?
- When are we going to get married?
- When are you going to stop drinking with your friends?
- Are you going to watch the football AGAIN tonight?
- Is my sister prettier than me?
- How many women have you slept with?
- How much do you earn?

Arguing in public

Under no circumstances should you ever argue in front of other people or in a public place. If you feel an argument coming on, change the subject and wait until a suitable moment arrives when you're on your own. The same applies to making snide and sarcastic remarks to one another.

When it's over

If you're planning to end a romance, try to arrange a meeting so you can do it in person, but if you think the situation could turn nasty, then choose a coffee shop or bar to break the news. If meeting is impossible, then at least telephone—failing that, a note explaining your feelings is the next best option. Never break up with someone by fax, email or text message. Make your explanation final; it's poor form to let someone think there may be another chance when you know there won't be. If you've met someone else, you should be discreet about beginning the new relationship to avoid further hurt and humiliation. And don't discuss why you've broken up with someone, except perhaps, with your parents, sister, brother or best friend.

LIVING WITH OTHERS

Whether you're in a relationship and living together or sharing accommodation, it's very important to respect one another's privacy and property. Matters of bills, the bond, cleaning duties, food, alcohol, and overnight guests should all be discussed upfront to avoid misunderstandings and arguments.

Never borrow food or alcohol from your flatmate's shelf in the refrigerator without checking that they're not keeping it to impress that Special Someone they're bringing home later that night. If you want to eat their food or drink their alcohol, ask first and then replace it as soon as you can.

As far as inviting that Special Someone to stay overnight goes, if they're in your flatmate's bedroom and don't commandeer the communal bathroom or eat you out of house and home, it shouldn't be a problem for you—unless, of course, they're becoming a permanent fixture. In this case, you need to discuss their contribution to the food bill and the phone bill. If they, in turn, start inviting their friends to drop by, then you may need to re-evaluate whether this is going to work for all of you.

Chapter 7

ENGAGEMENTS AND WEDDING PREPARATIONS

Before you make the big decision to get married, take your mind off the shower tea and that exotic honeymoon and think about the actual marriage itself. Are you signing a pre-nuptial agreement? Will you continue to work? How many children would you both like? You should also discuss money—will you have a joint bank account, buy a house or rent? The list is endless, but all these issues, and more, should be addressed before you get married. If you agree on most points and feel you are both on the same track in life, then the next thing to do is to plan your wedding.

Many couples prefer a quiet announcement that they've decided to get married. If it's a second marriage, any children from either of the previous marriages should be told first, and as soon as possible, with each parent responsible for telling his or her own offspring.

If it's a first marriage, then it's important that the woman's family is the first to be told—particularly since while it's no longer considered necessary for a man to ask his prospective father-in-law for his daughter's hand in marriage, the bride's parents are still traditionally the ones who will pay for the wedding.

Next, the bridegroom's parents should be told. If the two families have never met, then it would be a good idea at this time to arrange for drinks, lunch or dinner so that they can get to know one another. This may also be the time to organise another gathering where any other relatives and friends can be told.

If either of the engaged couple is widowed or divorced, it's courteous and wise to make sure that former parents-in-law know of this union-to-be, especially if your children (and the in-laws' grandchildren), are involved. Many older people become distressed if they find out about an engagement through the newspaper.

The idea of an engagement is to give both people involved time to prepare for the wedding, so the duration of the engagement will usually be dictated, in part, by how elaborate the wedding will be. However today, other factors come into play, such as paying off a unit in which the young couple intend to live or, in the case of a couple marrying for the second time, giving the children of both parties time to adjust to the idea of their parents remarrying.

HOW TO ANNOUNCE AN ENGAGEMENT

A notice in the personal column of your daily newspaper is inexpensive. You fill in a form at the local newsagency, both sign it in front of the newsagent, who then phones it through to the newspaper. Family and friends interstate and overseas can be notified by email, facsimile, telephone or post.

SAMPLE ENGAGEMENT ANNOUNCEMENT

Mr and Mrs Curtis Jones of St Ives have pleasure in announcing the engagement of their youngest daughter, Elizabeth to Peter, the only child of Mr and Mrs Len Smith of Rockhampton.

The couple can host an engagement party and share the cost or the bride's parents may like to host a party.

If this were to be a subsequent marriage for the couple, a small dinner party for close family and friends would be an appropriate way to announce the engagement.

If one of the parents is deceased, the notice would be as follows:

SAMPLE ANNOUNCEMENT WITH DECEASED PARENT

Jones–Smith

Phillip and Susan Jones of St Ives
are pleased to announce the engagement of their
youngest daughter, Elizabeth to Peter, only child of
Marilyn Smith and the late Albert Smith of Penrith.

If the parents are divorced and one has remarried, the appropriate notice would be as follows:

SAMPLE ANNOUNCEMENT WITH DIVORCED PARENTS

Richardson–Jones

Mr Albert Richardson of Toorak and Mrs Marilyn Smith of Newcastle are pleased to announce the engagement of their only child, Elizabeth to Peter, youngest son of Mr Phillip Jones of St Ives and Mrs May Atwill of Ascot.

Choosing an engagement ring

It's accepted that the man pays for the engagement ring, but many young women now prefer to choose their own ring and couples even share the cost—particularly if the ring chosen is more costly than the bridegroom-to-be had expected. Many couples ignore the engagement ring and invest in a more expensive wedding ring perhaps set with precious stones. In either case, make sure you get a valuation certificate from the jeweller and insure your rings against damage or loss. A photograph can be useful if the ring is stolen.

Birthstones

If you have a birthstone of which you are particularly fond you may want to think of the following for your engagement ring:

Month	Stone	Character
January	garnet	constancy
February	amethyst	sincerity
March	bloodstone	courage
April	diamond	purity
May	emerald	hope
June	agate or pearl	good health
July	ruby	passion
August	sardonyx	married happiness

September	sapphire	repentance
October	opal	lovableness
November	topaz	cheerfulness
December	turquoise	unselfishness

To party or not to party?

If there is an engagement party, it's usual for the bride's parents to host it and it would be diplomatic to arrange for the two sets of parents to meet before the party so that a joint guest list can be compiled. These days, it's usual for the bridegroom's parents to offer to pay for the alcohol and in some cases to share in the cost of the entire occasion. If you find that there are many relatives and older people on both sides, why not have two parties? If there's to be just a sprinkling of people in different age groups and most of the guests would blend in well together, go ahead with one party. If you keep to a cocktail party or casual buffet meal then people will mingle, which is what you want the two prospective families to do.

Engagement toast

If the engagement party has a buffet meal, then keep your toast very short. Remember, a lot of female guests may be balancing precariously on five-inch heels!

SAMPLE ENGAGEMENT TOAST

Simon is a fine young man and we look forward to welcoming him into our family. I'd also like to thank Simon's parents for their kind words about Annabelle earlier this evening.

Everyone will raise their glasses and say, 'To Annabelle and Simon'.

Depending on the formality of the occasion, Annabelle may wish to respond:

'Shower' parties or kitchen teas

The rationale behind 'showers' is that guests who aren't attending the wedding are invited and bring gifts to help set the young couple up in their new home. A 'shower' can be, for example, a linen shower, a bedroom shower or a cellar shower. If the bride-to-be has not lived away from home, then she may choose to have a kitchen tea where guests give items for the kitchen as gifts. These events are particularly relevant if the wedding is to be small, as it gives uninvited friends, neighbours and extended family an opportunity to be involved.

'Showers' can be hosted by the mother of the bride or bridegroom-to-be, a sister, a bridesmaid, or indeed, all of the bridesmaids can get together and host a 'shower'. If most of the bride-to-be's friends work, then an evening or weekend is preferable.

By the time 'showers' are planned, the bride-to-be will usually have selected her attendants, so if in doubt as to what to take, ring either the bride's mother (who will know if there is a bridal gift register), or one of the bridesmaids; it's safer than giving something that the bride doesn't need.

'Showers' would normally not be held for a bride marrying for the second or third time, as the purpose of a 'shower' is to provide the bride with equipment necessary to make a home. If, however, many of the bride's possessions were distributed to her previous partner in the divorce settlement, then her friends may wish to host a 'shower' for her again.

Buck's and hen's nights

For both the bride and the bridegroom, pre-wedding parties are customary. The bridesmaids, a friend of the mother of the bride, a godmother, or perhaps a group of friends who are unable to attend the wedding would usually host these parties. Some brides organise a 'hen's weekend' away where the bride and her attendants rent an apartment or hotel suite and party on for the bride's last weekend as a single woman. Similarly, a private room in a restaurant can be booked and the party held there.

Apart from the bridesmaids (who may be invited), it's preferable not to invite people who are already attending the wedding as it puts them in the position of having to buy yet another gift—remembering they have probably already bought an engagement gift.

For the bridegroom, the best man usually organises a 'buck's night' at a restaurant or club.

How to break off an engagement

A broken engagement is painful and an entirely personal matter, so under *no* circumstances should the couple be pressured to discuss the reasons for the break-up.

The woman is responsible for returning the gifts sent to her by her friends or family, and the man for gifts given by his. If the man has instigated the end of the relationship, the woman may keep the ring (unless it is a family heirloom), in which case it may be redesigned or worn on another finger. Usually, however, if the woman has decided to the end the relationship, she would return the ring to her former fiancé. If it were a mutual decision to end the relationship and the man paid for the ring, he would keep it; however, if they bought it together, perhaps it could be sold and both parties reimbursed, or one party could purchase it from the other party.

It's not really necessary to make a newspaper announcement unless both parties feel too distressed to make phone calls or write personal notes. Even then, a parent or close friend, best man or chief bridesmaid, aunt or godmother could assist in making the calls. If the wedding is quite close when the engagement is broken off, the parents of the bride-to-be should phone or write to the guests. Simply explain that the wedding will now not be going ahead and thank guests for their gift, which of course, will be returned.

If you feel that, because of the numbers of people involved and the embarrassment you are feeling, you prefer to put an announcement in the paper, you could state that:

SAMPLE BROKEN ENGAGEMENT ANNOUNCEMENT

Mr and Mrs Charles Taylor of St Adelaide regret to announce that the marriage of their daughter, Cherlyn, to Mr Adam Malouf of Port Pirie, will no longer take place.

It is usual for the party who broke off the engagement to cover or contribute to lost deposits. If the decision is mutual, costs should be shared.

PLANNING THE WEDDING

A wedding is a legal and formal acknowledgement of the life commitment a couple wish to enter into and a celebration of their love. To make the day successful and special, it's best to be clear on what your own personal wishes are for the day and what responsibilities people have during the event.

Pre-nuptial agreements or marriage contracts

Pre-nuptial agreements may be taken out to assist partners in the proper recording of assets brought into the marriage. Of course, if the marriage is short, the strength of the pre-nuptial agreement will be greater in order to reflect an accurate starting point for the division of marital property in proportion to the pro-rata values originally contributed to the marriage.

With long marriages the reliability of pre-nuptial agreements is diluted, as many factors relating to the joint acquisition of assets and financial contributions will cloud their proper division.

Remember that the Family Court has extremely wide powers and may overturn any arrangement, including pre-nuptials, to award a fair settlement to both parties.

Paying for a wedding

Many weddings are very costly; traditionally, the bride's parents arranged both the wedding and the reception and pay for just about everything that went into making it. This arrangement is frequently modified today.

What should the bride's family pay for?

The bride's family will usually pay for:

- hire of a venue, hotel or reception house
- caterers
- drinks
- the wedding cake
- flowers for the church, reception and bridesmaids' bouquets
- car hire from the bride's home to the ceremony and from the ceremony to the reception house or hotel, unless this is one of the items that the bridegroom or his parents have suggested they pay for
- the organist, choir or soloist at the ceremony
- the music at the reception (band or disk jockey)
- the printing and mailing of wedding invitations (see pages 14–19)
- any newspaper announcements
- both engagement and wedding photographs.

What should the bridegroom's family pay for?

Traditionally, the bridegroom's family has not been involved, but in recent years it's become common practice for the bridegroom's parents to either:

- pay for the purchase of liquor for the reception
- pay the cost of all music at the reception, or
- offer to pay half of the reception costs—particularly if they have an extended family and know they will be inviting more than half of the guests.

What should the bridegroom pay for?

The bridegroom would usually pay for:

- any church fees
- the bride's wedding ring
- the bride's bouquet
- a wedding gift for the bride
- buttonhole flowers for himself, his best man and the ushers
- the marriage licence
- transport from the ceremony to the reception
- corsages for his mother and the bride's mother
- gifts for his attendants, best man, groomsmen and ushers
- gifts for the flower girls and pageboys if there are any
- gifts for the bridal attendants or bridesmaids.

What should the bride pay for?
Traditionally, even the bride's gown was bought by the bride's parents, and some families still prefer to do this, but many brides today choose to purchase their own gown. Sometimes, the bride may offer to pay for half of each bridesmaid's dress or for dress-making costs and provide their dress fabric or accessories.

If wedding rings are to be exchanged, the bride also pays for the bridegroom's ring and she will usually buy a gift for the bridegroom.

What does the best man pay for?
Nothing. The best man's role is to be responsible for the wedding rings on the day and before that he is usually the one to organise the bridegroom's 'buck's party'.

What do the bridesmaids pay for?
Customarily, the bride paid for the bridesmaids' and matron of honour's dresses and shoes, but today the cost is often shared. If the bridesmaids do have to pay for their dresses, the decision on the style of dress is also shared so that the bridesmaids can choose a dress that they feel comfortable wearing after the wedding.

If the bride insists her attendants wear a distinctive colour or style and it's something that they won't be likely to wear later, then she should pay for the dresses and any accessories required.

The role of bridesmaids, groomsmen and attendants

The bridesmaids, groomsmen and attendants all have important roles to play on the wedding day. It can be tactful to include a member of the bridegroom's family in the bridal party, particularly if he has only one sister, young sisters who could be flower girls, or little brothers who could serve as pageboys.

If the bride is marrying for the second or third time, then she may choose a friend of many years standing, a sister or a close relative, as her attendant.

Chief bridesmaid or matron of honour

The chief bridesmaid or matron of honour will:
- keep the younger attendants under control
- help the bride dress and keep her calm
- look after the wedding rings until they are handed to the best man before the ceremony
- be a witness to the union and sign the marriage cerificate
- assist the bridegroom in choosing gifts for the other bridesmaids
- arrange a 'shower' or kitchen tea
- assist the bride in planning what to take on her honeymoon and help her pack
- hand out the wedding cake and oversee the task of sending wedding cake to guests who were unable to attend the wedding
- gather the gifts together and ensure that they make it to the bride's home safely.

Bridesmaids

Bridesmaids should:
- keep in touch with the bride to see if there's anything they can do in the way of running around and helping out
- assist the bride and her mother in addressing envelopes and sticking on stamps
- co-host a 'shower' or kitchen tea for the bride and invite the bride's female friends and family members
- circulate and make sure that interstate or older guests are not left standing lost and alone at the reception

- assist the chief bridesmaid or matron of honour in handing out slices of wedding cake.

Best man
The best man should:
- organise the bachelor dinner or buck's party to which friends of the bridegroom, the bride's brothers (if any) and other grooms-men or ushers are invited
- choose and buy a collective present for the bridegroom
- make sure the bridegroom has any required paperwork and airline tickets on hand on the day of the wedding
- arrive at the bridegroom's home early on the wedding day to help him to dress and to assist with any problems that may arise
- be a witness to the union and sign the marriage certificate
- make sure that the bridegroom arrives at the church in time, and confirm any transport arrangements
- hand over the wedding rings during the ceremony
- ensure that cheques or cash have been put in envelopes ready for discreet payment of the minister, organist or choir
- make the second toast at the reception
- invite all of the female members of the bridal party to dance, and then ask the mother of the bride and the mother of the bride-groom to dance.

Flower girls and pageboys
If the bride has a long train, flower girls and pageboys may help to carry it over the church steps; some brides have them stand near the bridal party with the wedding rings on satin cushions ready to be exchanged.

Ushers
Ushers should:
- make sure everyone is seated correctly; it would be wise to have one usher per every fifty wedding guests
- greet the guests as they arrive, so it's preferable if they do have some idea of who's who

- hand out the service sheets and show the guests to their seats
- assist at the last minute if there are any hitches
- watch for the mother of the bride and seat her; another usher will take care of the mother of the bridegroom
- make sure that everyone has transport to the reception
- dance with the bride and with each of the bride's attendants, and perhaps even with the mother of the bride and the mother of the bridegroom.

What do the bride's parents do?

The mother of the bride should:
- decide which of their friends will be invited to the wedding
- arrange for the printing of the invitations, although the style of the invitation is a joint decision between her and her daughter
- enlist a close friend to help her write out the envelopes and stick on the stamps
- enter the acceptances into the guest list
- follow up those who have not replied
- plan the seating for the reception
- go to the church in a hired car, perhaps with the bridesmaids, or with a male member of the family who will escort her up the aisle
- act as host, greeting the wedding party and the guests as they arrive at the reception.

When the mother of the bride sits, it's a signal for the bride to enter the church with her attendants.

If for some reason, there's no male person to give the bride away, it's correct for the mother of the bride to do so. Similarly, in cases where the daughter has been brought up single-handedly by her mother, it's not uncommon for the mother to give her daughter away. If the father is still in contact with his daughter, she may still choose to ask her father to give her away, but it's not uncommon for mother and father to jointly escort their daughter to the altar.

The father of the bride should escort the bride down the aisle and 'give her away' at the altar, and then sit down beside the mother of the bride in the front pew.

If the father of the bride is deceased, his role may be taken by a stepfather, uncle, brother, godfather or close friend of the bride.

Who sits where?

The bride's friends and family will be seated on the left of the aisle as you walk into the church, and the friends and family of the bride-groom will be seated on the right.

If parents are divorced, it's usual for them to be seated together at the ceremony (their new partners, if there are any, aren't part of the 'official' wedding party and will sit a few pews behind with friends). The parents may sit with their new partners at the reception.

Wedding rings

Today many couples exchange rings and it's customary to go together to choose them before the wedding. Rings are exchanged during the ceremony and can be carried by a pageboy or a flower girl who would stand with the couple at the altar ready to pass over the rings, which usually sit on velvet or satin cushions. If there are no flower girls or pageboys, the best man is usually entrusted to keep the rings until they're exchanged

Traditionally, wedding rings were a simple band of gold, but today many brides choose to have precious stones in the ring instead of having a separate engagement ring. Matching 'his and hers' rings are also gaining popularity.

Limousine hire

Some couples on a limited budget accept the generosity of friends who may offer the use of a smart car for the bridal party on the day. Some brides choose to decorate the bridesmaids' car in the same colours that the bridesmaids are wearing, leaving white decoration for the bride's car only.

If limousine hire cars are to be used, comparative quotes should be sought and the booking made early. Remember that because Saturday afternoon and evenings are prime time for the limousine industry, an extension of time is often not possible as the driver may have another wedding afterwards. If, however, the driver has no other booking after yours, he may agree to stay, although most companies will charge waiting time (at approximately $50.00 per hour). If you have a car waiting, it's important to liaise with your photographer to ensure that photographic sessions don't run on and on.

Flowers for the wedding party

Choice will depend on the style of the bride's dress and the height and build of the bride. Some brides prefer silk flowers, which can be kept as a memento of the day. Flowers for the matron of honour or chief bridesmaid, other bridesmaids and flower girls should all complement the bouquet chosen by the bride. The men usually wear boutonnières (buttonholes), that is, a single flower which goes through the buttonhole in the lapel of the man's suit, and corsages should be ordered for the two mothers. It's preferable to work with only one florist so that everything is matching and arrives at the house at the same time.

Flowers for the church

Decorating the church is usually carried out by either the bride's and bridegroom's mothers, or perhaps a godmother or close friend who has a flair for floral arrangement. Much will depend on the size and grandeur of the church but, in any case, decoration can either single flowers, posies or ribbons attached to the end of the pews and should complement the colour of the bride's gown and those of her attendants.

Bridal wear

What the bride wears is up to her budget, her sense of style, and her desire to be different, as well as the kind of wedding she has chosen to have.

Modern day brides may wear whatever takes their fancy. Traditionally, brides wear white, and even if a couple has lived together for some time before marriage, the bride may still choose to wear white.

If white doesn't suit you then, of course, any pastel colour is appropriate. If you want to stay close to white then magnolia, cream or ivory are lovely. If the bride chooses to wear a veil, then it should be covering her face on the way to the church and down the aisle. The bridegroom then lifts the veil in order to kiss the bride after they exchange vows.

Trains are popular, particularly if the bride has chosen to have flower girls and pageboys to carry it. Obviously much depends on the grandeur of the wedding as well as your budget and how effectively you can carry off the full regalia. Bear in mind that you'll be wearing your wedding dress at the reception, so you should be able to not only dance in it, but also move around comfortably chatting to guests.

If a bride is marrying for the second, third or subsequent time, she can be as conventional as she likes (but would usually avoid the virginal veil over the face), or can dress casually in a pantsuit. What she chooses to wear will depend on how formal a wedding she wants.

If the bridegroom gives the bride a gift, for example a string of pearls, it would be appropriate to wear them at the wedding. The bridesmaids, the mother of the bride, the bridegroom's mother, or even just friends enjoy giving the bride the 'something old, something new, something borrowed and something blue' to be worn on the day.

What the bride chooses to wear, and the time of day of the wedding, will determine what the bridegroom, best man, grooms-men and guests will wear.

What to wear for a morning wedding

If the wedding takes place before lunch, the bride could wear a short dress—although long is more popular—and the bridegroom would wear a morning suit. A grey cravat can be substituted for a tie if desired and a black cravat is often worn after midday.

Male guests attending a morning wedding should wear a lounge suit with a tie, and women guests can wear anything from a suit, a dress with a jacket, or an elegant dress. This is the kind of wedding where women could lash out and wear a big hat.

What to wear for an afternoon wedding

If the wedding takes place in the afternoon, the bride could still wear a long dress with a shorter veil, or a short dress with a hat.

Ribbons or fresh flowers are suitable for a younger bride, as is an elaborate wedding gown with a long train and veil. The men in the wedding party would wear dark lounge suits and ties.

Male guests attending an afternoon wedding could also wear the same as the groomsmen, while women would wear the same as for a formal morning wedding.

What to wear for an evening wedding

The bridegroom could wear a dinner suit and black tie. For those men who like to be more adventurous they can choose trendy shirts and ties, cummerbunds or waistcoats. It can be attractive if the men's ties match the bridesmaids' dresses. Instead of a bow tie, many young men now favour a black V-tie, or a coloured tie to match their lapel flower (the boutonnière) or the bridesmaids' dresses. Males in the wedding party should also wear black tie.

Male guests attending an evening wedding should wear a dinner suit; otherwise, they should wear a dark lounge suit and tie.

Women can afford to be more adventurous at this time of the day, and cocktail dresses, dinner dresses, or even short evening dresses can be worn.

What to wear for a registry office wedding

If the wedding is to be at a registry office, the bride could wear a suit, pantsuit, a short dress or a wedding dress. She would probably choose a small posy rather than a long, trailing bouquet. The groomsmen could wear lounge suits, or perhaps jackets with ties.

Wedding traditions

In the 14th century, it was a common wedding 'sport' for the bride to toss her garter (a symbol of good luck) to the men. However, it was soon found that sometimes the men—having had a bit too much to drink—would try to remove the garter themselves ahead of time! To put an end to that misbehaviour, it became customary for the bridegroom to remove the garter and toss it to the men. It's thought to be at this time that the bride started to toss the bridal bouquet to the unwed girls of marriageable age.

Horseshoes are commonly worn by brides and are an ancient symbol of fertility. Carrying a horseshoe is said to bring good luck, but the horseshoe must be carried with the 'U' shape pointing upwards to 'keep the luck in'.

Shoes symbolise fertility and when tied to the back of the newlyweds' car signify recognition of a new family unit being created.

Brides carry a handkerchief as a lucky sign.

'Something old, something new, something borrowed and something blue' is another tradition followed by brides on their wedding day. Something old represents something old with the family of her childhood. Something new represents the new life ahead. Something borrowed represents reliance and the help of friends. Something blue represents faithfulness and trust and stems from ancient Israel where blue denoted fidelity and love.

Wedding gifts

These days many brides leave a 'gift list' or 'bridal registry' at major department stores; if this is the case, it will usually be mentioned in the wedding invitation. If it's not mentioned, ask the bride's mother and contact the store to have the list posted or faxed to you. Prices are always included on these lists, so you can choose a gift that meets your budget.

If your friend or relative isn't being married for the first time, you should still give a wedding gift—unless the invitation specifies not to. Having said that, if you gave a very expensive wedding present to your friend at their first marriage you don't have to follow suit the second time around. You can attach a sincere note offering your well wishes. Even if you weren't invited to the second wedding, you should send a small gift with a note upon hearing news of the impending union.

Gift register

Some brides actually make out their own list, which they like to circulate to family and friends; others name the store where the item can be purchased. This sometimes offends older people, but for friends who are busy or those who don't know what to give, this can make the selection much easier as the stores can also gift-wrap and deliver.

Where do you take the gift?

It has always been considered best not to take gifts to the church, but rather to take them to the home of the bride before the wedding. If guests are travelling from interstate or overseas, it may be difficult to make a special trip to the bride's home. As mentioned above, out of town guests can order gifts by telephone or fax from the department store gift register and have them gift-wrapped and delivered.

Preferably, gifts should be sent to the bride's home. Even if you're a friend of the bridegroom, you don't send the gift to him. However, if the bride lives in the country but the bridegroom or his parents live in the city, it makes more sense to send the gift to his home. If this is not possible, take it to the reception and give it to the bridesmaids for safekeeping. Under no circumstances should you hand the gift to the couple themselves.

Make sure your gift is well labelled with your name or a card that cannot fall off, that way you can be thanked.

Remember, if you receive an invitation to a wedding and you can't go, it's still customary to send a gift.

Thank you notes

The newlyweds should write their thank you notes as soon as possible after returning from their honeymoon. When opening the gifts, a list should be kept of who gave what so that mention can be made of the gift in the letter.

SAMPLE THANK YOU NOTE

Dear Cecily and Adrian,
We are so thrilled to receive your champagne goblets, which are absolutely beautiful.
  When we're settled in the new unit, we would like you to be our first dinner guests and we will christen them together.
  Many thanks for your generosity.
Fondest love,
Jessica and Mark Simpson

What if you're given identical gifts?

If you receive five woks, you can:

- keep one and put four on your 'gift shelf' to give away at the next four weddings you attend. If you do this, leave the giver's card on the present so that you don't give it back to them!
- ring those four guests and explain your dilemma and ask if they would mind if you exchanged it.

Important wedding anniversaries

1st	Paper
5th	Wood
10th	Tin
15th	Crystal
20th	China
25th	Silver
30th	Pearl
35th	Jade
40th	Ruby
45th	Sapphire
50th	Gold
55th	Emerald
60th	Diamond

Chapter 8

THE WEDDING CEREMONY
AND RECEPTION

Ironically, getting married can be even more stressful than getting divorced—not that I'm suggesting you try the latter so you can compare! Are you both over eighteen years of age? If not ... and you're female, you may still marry if both parents agree. The youngest age at which a girl may marry is fourteen, but this usually requires special circumstances (and a magistrate's consent).

If you're divorced and planning to re-marry, you'll need to provide your final divorce decree, known as the Decree Absolute. Different religions have different attitudes towards marrying previously divorced people.

If you're widowed and planning to re-marry, you'll need the death certificate of your previous partner.

If you were widowed and reverted to your single name, you could be married in that name; otherwise, you would be married under the surname of your deceased spouse (if that's the name you've been using). The 'widowed' bride is not usually 'given away' by her father, but is escorted to the church or restaurant (or wherever the ceremony is to take place) by her eldest son, brother, relative or close friend.

If you have children who were born out of wedlock this will not prevent you from having a religious ceremony but it's up to the discretion of the cleric or rabbi concerned whether or not he'll perform the ceremony.

If one of the people being married is an atheist, agnostic or a member of a different religion to the other, they may be asked to attend classes to familiarise themselves with the teachings of the faith of their partner's church or synagogue.

Finally, brides may either retain their maiden surname, or retain it and add their husband's surname to it, or adopt their husband's surname and drop their maiden name.

WHAT KIND OF WEDDING?

The next step is to decide what kind of wedding you want. Do you want:

- a religious wedding?
- a civil ceremony with a marriage celebrant?
- to be married at the registry office?

If you choose a religious or church wedding, approach the minister, rabbi or priest and make an appointment to discuss the ceremony. If the ceremony is to be with a marriage celebrant or at the registry office, do the same.

Whether it is a religious or civil marriage, you must obtain a 'Notice of Intended Marriage' (clergy have copies of this), and it must be given to the person who is to perform the ceremony no more than six months and not less than one calendar month and one day before the ceremony takes place.

RECORDING THE DAY

Many couples choose music that has sentimental significance for them. If you're not sure of what you want, conduct an Internet search using 'wedding music' as your subject.

Videos are filmed on a professional digital format and edited, come with special effects, titles, your choice of music, and hi-fi stereo sound. Many companies use radio lapel microphones to enhance the quality of sound during the vows and speeches at the reception. If you want to video a religious ceremony, you must ask permission from the minister, priest or rabbi beforehand.

Professional wedding photographs are usually considered a must. Photographs of the bride and her bridal party can be taken at any time according to the bride's wishes.

MANNERS FOR MARRYING MORE THAN ONCE

If you're on good terms with your previous spouse or ex-parents in-law, invite them too. It will make your children feel more comfortable and they'll find it easier to accept your new marriage if they see that both of their parents accept it.

If the parents are divorced and the father of the bride is anxious to be at the wedding, then the mother of the bride must do her best to overlook any differences she has and make a happy day of it. If the father of the bride doesn't wish to attend the wedding, or feels he can't be in the company of his ex-wife for so many hours, then it may be possible to organise a special dinner before the wedding where the father alone, or with his new wife, attends with close friends of the bride and of her father. If time is of the essence, a dinner with one parent could even be arranged after the honeymoon.

This arrangement would also work if the mother had no objection to the father attending the wedding, but objected to his new wife being there. A compromise could be that the new wife attends the church ceremony but not the reception, or that she attends a dinner with her husband or stepchild but without the mother being present.

If, however, the parents are divorced and the father has started a new life in which his first family plays no part, then the mother would be the one to announce the engagement, host the engagement party (if there is one), issue invitations, and be the host on the occasion of the wedding.

Another option is for the father to give the bride away in the church and be there for the official photographs, but not attend the reception afterwards.

Yet another possibility is for both parents to accompany the bride to 'give her away'. This is an excellent solution where, although the father is the traditional parent to 'give the daughter away', the mother has been responsible for the daughter's upbringing.

If the mother of the bride has remarried and her new husband has been responsible for bringing the daughter up as his own, then it would be worth considering coming to an understanding with the natural father. Perhaps the stepfather's name could be on the wedding invitation, particularly if he's to give the bride away and pay for the wedding.

Often a simple phone call will clarify matters. Much will depend on the degree of amicability between parents. However it is to be done, all arrangements should be made well beforehand so that no arguments spoil the bride's day.

THE WEDDING RECEPTION

The kind of reception you have will depend on how much money you or your parents wish to spend and what time of day you choose to have the wedding ceremony. It's wise to select a venue near where the ceremony was held so it's conveniently located for your guests.

A morning wedding will lend itself to a luncheon afterwards. An early afternoon wedding—say 2.00 p.m.—would be the ideal time to have an afternoon tea, which has the advantages of less alcohol being served and a less expensive menu. A late afternoon wedding would be ideal for a cocktail party. An evening wedding—say 6.00 p.m.—would generally mean dinner, which can be either a buffet or a sit-down dinner.

At the reception

Since the bride's parents are the official hosts for the day, they would normally stand at the head of the line—the mother first and then the father. After the bride's parents come the bridegroom's parents—his mother first and then his father—and then the bride and bridegroom. At this time the bridal attendants, both hers and his, should be acting as unofficial hosts—introducing guests to one another, taking gifts from those guests who've brought them, making sure that drinks are being served and watching the behaviour of the small attendants, if there are any.

At a less formal reception many couples prefer to greet the guests themselves, leaving the parents of the bride and bridegroom free to circulate with the guests. A receiving line can be awkward if there are step-parents who have been very involved in the upbringing of the bride or bridegroom. If this is the case, eliminate this formality.

Who will sit where?

Unless the step-parent has been actively involved in raising the bride or bridegroom, they are not part of the bridal party and should be seated with the other guests.

You can notify your guests of where to sit either by a notice at the door of the dining room or by place cards in position on the table. The bride and bridegroom's parents should liaise so that if either family has one or two difficult relatives they'll know where best to place them. Very often, the bridegroom's friends and family don't know any of the bride's friends and family, so you have the options of seating all of the bride's friends and family together, and all of the bridegroom's friends and family together; or mixing them.

The second option can be risky if you are marrying someone from a different ethnic background, especially if his or her friends and family speak little or no English. If that's the case, seat the family together so that no-one feels uncomfortable because everyone around them is speaking in a foreign tongue.

If you do decide to mix friends from both families (and each table seats eight), you could have two couples from each side of the family at each table, providing a nice balance.

How to seat the bridal party

Usually only the bride and bridegroom and their attendants sit at the bridal table. The bride and bridegroom sit in the middle, and working left from the bridegroom would be the best man and groomsmen, while on the right of the bride would be her matron of honour and her other bridesmaids. If there are flower girls and pageboys, depending on their age and how well behaved they are, they're best kept at the table with their parents.

The parents of the bride and bridegroom would host their own tables of close relatives and friends. If the two families know each other well and get along, they may choose to co-host a table of close or elderly relatives. Either of these options makes it easier if there are divorced couples involved and, in a case like this, if the new wife were on good terms with the mother of the bride, then she could be included at this table; otherwise, she would sit with friends at another table.

If the father of the bride or bridegroom is deceased, divorced or living out of the country, it's best for the mother to host a table so she doesn't feel alone. Similarly, if a friend of the family, a godfather, or an older brother gave the bride away, this person may choose to sit at the official table with the bridal party; but if he has a partner of his own, then he may elect to sit with her. If, for example, the bride's brother gave her away, he may want to go back and sit with his wife; in which case, if the minister or priest has been invited to attend the reception and the bride's mother is widowed, the priest may well sit beside her.

If, for any reason, the bridegroom's parents were hosting the wedding (for example if the bride comes from overseas or has no family), only the bridal party would sit at the bridal table.

Entertainment at the reception

An MC (master or mistress of ceremonies) can be employed by the bridal party to ensure the smooth running of the reception. A good MC will:

- introduce him or herself to the audience and put them and the bridal party at ease
- introduce those who make a toast or a wedding speech
- act as timekeeper for people who do make speeches
- thank the previous speaker and introduce the next.

Music

Music should be background only when guests are eating and talking—perhaps a pianist, a violinist, a harpsichordist, an accordionist or a wandering minstrel, which could be interesting and different. If you plan to include dancing in the festivities, then you can hire a band or DJ. Most musicians welcome a list of songs selected by the bride and groom to play throughout the evening.

Speeches and toasts

Making the speeches at the beginning of the reception prevents people having too many drinks before they say their 'few words' and also saves those who are making speeches from sitting rigid with fear waiting for their moment to come. All speakers should be reminded to keep it brief, relevant and tasteful.

Glasses should be filled and people on their feet before the toast is proposed. If no waiters are present, guests could be asked to charge their own glasses. Those who don't drink wine can raise a glass of water for the toast.

At the beginning of the dessert course, the host may propose a toast to the bride and groom; at this time, it is tradition that the host stand. The bride and groom to whom the toast is proposed should remain seated and should not drink the toast.

The groom should then rise and respond with a toast, to which they also may drink. This is when other guests might rise and propose toasts of their own. It would be wise for the MC to advise them beforehand on the wisdom of brevity.

The father of the bride usually makes the toast to the bride and bridegroom. If the bride's father has passed away or is absent, a relative or close family friend will toast instead.

The father of the groom makes a toast to the bride and bridegroom.

The bridegroom would then toast the bridesmaids, and the best man would usually respond on behalf of the bridesmaids.

Nowadays, the bride may respond to a toast instead of her new husband.

The chief bridesmaid may decide to respond on behalf of the other bridesmaids, or if any one of the bridesmaids is a competent speaker, she may be elected to speak on their behalf.

The mother of the bride may also be the one to toast the couple.

Note: The MC should be ready to intervene if any of the speakers embarks on a lengthy monologue.

Your wedding cake

If you depart from tradition and choose a croquembouche (which should be stored in a cool place) or ice-cream cake (which should be stored in the deep freeze), it can double as dessert, so let the caterers know where to put them when they arrive. It's traditional to save the top tier of the wedding cake for the baptism of the first child; if you want to uphold this tradition, again remind the caterers beforehand.

After the cutting of the cake and the bridal waltz, the bride and bridegroom should do their best to circulate amongst the guests.

When to leave the reception

The MC or best man should be told well beforehand what time the couple intend to leave. Guests shouldn't leave until after the newly-married couple do, so it is up to the MC or best man to keep to the schedule.

Receptions for a second, third—or even fourth!—wedding

If this isn't your first wedding, it's most likely that you will be opting for a more casual kind of reception—perhaps lunch in a restaurant, or even a dinner or buffet meal at a hotel or reception house. In any case, you'll probably modify the ceremony and the reception. You may still choose to have speeches, a wedding cake and dancing, but the formality and protocol may not be necessary.

Usually, couples marrying for the second or subsequent time would request that no gifts be given, but if guests feel more comfortable doing so, then the same rule applies. Thank you notes should be attended to promptly and guests should make sure that their gifts are properly labelled.

For this kind of wedding, unless the groom is particularly affluent and wants to pay for everything, the couple would usually split the cost between them. Rarely should parents be asked to fork out again for another wedding, but if the father of the bride wants to pay again then he should be allowed to do so.

If there are children from either of the previous marriages, they should be involved (only if they want to, of course), and be encouraged to feel important on the day. For this kind of wedding, there will probably be no formal photographs taken beforehand, rather, informal snaps throughout the wedding and reception and perhaps a video if the couple so desire.

Chapter 9
BIRTHS, DIVORCES AND DEATHS

Just as a birth is a happy event and certain traditional steps are usually taken to announce it, divorces and deaths also need to be made known publicly with decorum and respect.

WHEN A CHILD IS BORN

As soon as it's convenient after the arrival of the child, the new father should inform both sets of grandparents, other family members and then close friends of the birth. If the mother is unmarried, she'll be the one to tell her parents. Depending on the unmarried mother's relationship with the parents of the child's father, she may, as a courtesy, let them know in addition to other close family and friends; or she may ask a sister or friend to make the calls for her.

It's customary to place a notice in the 'Births, Deaths and Marriages' (sometimes called Personal Notices) page of the local paper. This should include:

- the last name of the parents
- the sex of the baby
- the date and place of birth
- the mother's first name
- the mother's maiden name (for example, née Ward)
- the father's first name
- the name of the baby (if one has been chosen).

The birth must be registered with the Registry of Births, Deaths and Marriages; this procedure is not only required by law but is necessary if the child needs a passport, marriage licence or anything where proof of age is required later in life.

The hospital will usually provide the form but if it doesn't, forms can be obtained from the office of the Registry of Births, Deaths and Marriages. Only one parent needs to sign the birth form.

If the parents of the child aren't married, and if you want both names to be on the birth form, you must provide a signed statutory declaration from *both the mother and father* consenting to the father's name being on the form.

If you're a single mother you can give *your* details only, *but* if you want (and the father wants), both names on the birth form, the same rule applies—you must *both* sign a statutory declaration.

Naming your child

Here are some good tips to follow when deciding on a name for your child:

- make sure your choice of first name sits well with your surname, e.g. Donald Donaldson will be hard to understand on the telephone
- watch the initials don't make up an unfavourable word, e.g. Mary Anne Donaldson (MAD)
- unisexual names like 'Leigh', 'Lee', 'Lindsay', 'Lesley', 'Sandy' or 'Sam' can be confusing later in life
- names like 'Indiana' or 'Idaho' could be a burden
- names like 'Honesty', 'Chastity', 'Charity', 'Virtue' and 'Trinity' could be an even heavier burden, especially if your child's nature doesn't match their name.

Baptism and naming ceremonies

Details vary from church to church, but usually involves the pouring of holy water on the baby's head three times—in the name of the Father, the Son and the Holy Spirit. If baptism is carried out later in life, the procedure remains the same.

It is not a legal or compulsory procedure so it's up to the parents as to when, if ever, a baptism should take place. Usually baptism takes place in a church of the religion to which you belong—presumably parents will want their children to practice the same religion. If you are not a member on any specific church, but your spouse or partner is a regular churchgoer, then you may choose their church.

A naming ceremony is a non-religious service formalising the name of a child and is usually performed by a celebrant. Naming ceremonies are commonly held in a garden or park, at a restaurant or on a boat and can be at any time of the day. There are sponsors instead of godparents and the wording of the ceremony can be individual and in any language you choose.

The party afterwards

The party can be for drinks, lunch or afternoon tea—depending on when the ceremony took place—and it's customary to invite the minister or priest to attend.

The top tier from the wedding cake, presuming it has been kept kept, is now produced and a toast drunk in champagne to the health and future of the baby.

What should the baby wear?

Traditionally, a baby wore white (symbolising purity) to their baptism, but today any colour is acceptable.

What should the parents wear?

This will depend on where the baptism is held. A formal baptism in a church with a lunch at a five-star hotel would require a jacket for the men and perhaps a dress or suit for the women. For a baptism in the garden or a naming ceremony with drinks to follow, more casual clothing is considered appropriate.

Gifts for the child

Gifts should be something that can be kept as a reminder of the occasion—godparents, however, may like to combine a gift and buy a small package of shares for the new child or open an account for the child's education or an insurance policy to mature on the child's 21st birthday. Otherwise a crucifix, a special book, a bible or prayer book, a family heirloom, a silver mug or a spoon set are appropriate.

IF YOU DIVORCE

When a couple separates with the view of getting divorced, it's extremely discourteous to ask why. It's up to them to tell you what they will—*when* they will and *if* they will.

It's wise to tell those who are immediately affected, such as grandparents, children, the school principal (who will pass it on the school counsellor), your bank manager, your accountant, and any others with whom you do business, for instance your home loan company. Others will find out soon enough.

If you are the one moving out of the marital home and there are many people to add to the list above, then a personal note or printed card is ideal. This serves the dual role of letting people know of the separation as well as giving your new address.

A divorced woman can choose to keep her husband's surname, but she should no longer refer to herself as Mrs Robert Edmonds, but as Mrs Jennifer Edmonds. Some younger women who have never adopted their husband's last name will remain as they were.

After the divorce, many women choose to revert to their maiden name. In this case, the children would keep the last name of their father, unless their relationship was very poor and much ill-feeling came about with the divorce, in which case older children may ask to change their surname to that of their mother.

'DOS' AND 'DON'TS' OF DIVORCING

- Do spend time with your closest friends and relatives and seek solace in their company.
- Don't give out the gory details to your friends or acquaintances—even if they ask!
- Do refrain from unduly criticising your partner, especially in front of your children.
- Do avoid gossiping about or setting out to destroy your partner's new relationships.
- Don't discuss with anyone else any financial concerns arising from the divorce or any custody cases being fought out in court.
- Do be discreet and only tell those who really need to know.

How to behave if your friends divorce

Friends often find they are in a difficult situation when a couple they know divorce. It is best that you:

- Don't take sides (especially if you're close to both people involved), and never criticise one in front of the other.
- Do keep in contact with both parties if they have both been good friends.
- Don't urge your friends to give you the details of the break-up.
- Do stop inviting one of them along if you're no longer friendly why torture yourself just to be impartial?
- Don't invite both partners to your home at the same time, unless they are on very good terms and have made it clear that they are happy to meet in this way.
- Don't ignore, ostracise or chastise the partner who re-marries soonest, even if they re-marry very soon after the divorce. There are two sides to every story so try to get along with their new partner and be impartial when the subject of your feelings is raised.

If you're the one instigating the divorce, it's up to you to engage a solicitor and tell your spouse you've done this with a view to beginning legal proceedings to end the marriage. Explain to the children what's happening and do your best to be calm and unemotional to help them to cope. If there is a third party involved, this isn't the time to bring them into the mix. The children may blame the break-up on them and this will make the acceptance of your new partner more difficult, if not impossible, later on. Keep a new relationship low-key and concentrate on ending your current relationship as amicably as possible.

It's a good idea to try to tie up as many financial commitments as you have and talk about how you'll divide any joint assets. These are difficult and trying times but they do pass. Consulting a counsellor could be beneficial, particularly if you think it would help the children. If one or both of you is having difficulty coming to terms with what has happened, a counsellor will be able to help you work through the range of emotions you're experiencing. It's very important that you don't 'bad mouth' your soon-to-be ex spouse and that you refrain from discussing the gory details with anyone. Very few people can be relied on not to repeat confidences whereas trained counsellors can. So be discreet.

DEATH

Death is inevitable for all of us and the most sensible thing we can do is to have a Will.

How do you make a Will?

A Will is a statement of what you want done with your assets after your death. The Public Trustee in all States will assist you and act as the Executor (a person appointed as an agent to carry out the terms after your death). A small fee is taken out of your estate for this service.

You may choose to write your Will yourself and take it to your solicitor to check it for 'loop holes' or you can go to your solicitor and have them prepare one for you. The solicitor may keep it in their office for safety. It is wise to make a new Will when you marry, divorce or have children.

If you have a collection of stamps, china, jewellery or antiques to be distributed amongst family members, make a list of who gets what to avoid confusion or squabbling.

What happens if you die without leaving a Will?

If you die without a Will, that is, intestate, your estate is divided according to the intestacy laws which will distribute your assets according to what the authorities presume you would have wanted. This can lead to ill-feeling and dissension among relatives.

Notifying the proper authorities of a death

The first step is to contact the deceased's doctor. If the deceased had been ill for a long time, the doctor treating him or her will have been aware of their condition and will issue a 'Medical Certificate of Cause of Death'. However, if the doctor has not attended the deceased person during the illness, or indeed has just been called and is unable to give a cause of death, then he or she must report the death to the police, who will contact the coroner.

If the deceased has died in a hospital, the hospital issues a 'Medical Certificate of Cause of Death'.

If the death was violent (as in a car accident, murder or suicide), then the police automatically contact the coroner's office as a post mortem (an examination of the body after death) or an inquest (an official inquiry into the probable cause of death) will usually be instigated. It is up to the coroner to authorise the funeral when the post mortem is complete. You could expect a delay of twenty-four to forty-eight hours before the funeral will proceed, plus the normal time span to organise the funeral. The coroner will issue a paper authorising a funeral director to collect the body for burial.

If the deceased person carried a donor card, contact a hospital as soon as possible—doing so may save someone else's life.

Who else should be contacted?

It is important to contact the following people once a death has occurred:

- minister, rabbi or priest
- the immediate family
- children and in-laws from any previous marriage
- close friends
- employer, business partners, or close colleagues
- the deceased's solicitor—you will need to ask if a Will existed and if it contained any special funeral requirements. The executor of the Will will ask you for the following:
    - financial records
    - bank passbooks
    - cheque books
    - property deeds
    - insurance/superannuation policies
    - tax returns
    - Medicare card numbers, and
    - share certificates.
- the deceased's accountant (often accounts or solicitors are named as executors in a Will)
- the deceased's insurance agent (the deceased may have a Life Insurance policy)
- the deceased's credit card company
- the deceased bank branch/s

- the Department of Veterans Affairs (if the deceased were an ex service person)
- the Department of Social Security (if the deceased were a pensioner their spouse may be eligible for a lump sum payout).

The quickest and easiest way to alert each of the above is to make phone calls. If you feel too distressed to do this, enlist the aid of a close friend.

You may also like to place a newspaper announcement, which must usually be reserved in the local paper before 5:00 p.m. on the day before publication. Unless the deceased had friends and business associates interstate, the notice need only be in a State-based metropolitan newspaper. The funeral director may also offer to place the notice for you. Often newspapers will only accept a Funeral Notice from a funeral director who conducts accounts with them (for identification purposes). Different papers have different rules.

You will need to make another announcement a few days later giving particulars of the funeral time and place; interested parties, having read the first announcement, will be watching for the second if they want to attend the funeral. This is when you would request donations to charity be made, rather than sending flowers, if that's what you want.

Since it's very stressful for the family when someone dies it can be very helpful for family or friends to take charge of:
- organising a babysitter to take care of any children
- answering incoming telephone calls and making a list of any flowers, gifts or sympathy messages
- organising a meal for the grieving friends and relatives.

Registering the death with the Registry of Births, Deaths & Marriages in your state

Generally the funeral director will complete the form and lodge it with the Registrar-General on behalf of the family. The formal, legal Death Certificate will be sent to the next of kin as directed on the application.

If you live a distance from the local registry or funeral director, the local police sergeant can act as the registrar. If the death was referred to the coroner, it can't be registered until the registrar receives authority from the coroner.

Whoever registers the death should either be the deceased's next of kin, a relative or a nominated person. The questions they will be asked are:

- the name of the deceased
- the age of the deceased
- the full name of the deceased's father
- the full name of the deceased's mother (and her maiden name)
- the date of death
- the address or place of death
- the deceased's address of permanent residence
- the occupation of the deceased
- the sex of the deceased
- the marital status of the deceased (and, if married, details of the marriage, including the date of the marriage and the partner's name)
- if the deceased were divorced (if so, you'll be asked details of the date of the divorce)
- if the deceased had any children, and if so, their names and ages
- your relationship to the deceased.

The funeral director adds details of the burial and signs the form and when this is done, the 'Information of Death Form' together with the Medical Certificate is sent to the local registrar and the death is registered. If the deceased has chosen cremation, the funeral director gives the particulars to the crematorium, which certifies that the body of the deceased has been cremated. Those forms are all forwarded to the Registrar for registration.

What else does a funeral director do?

Funeral directors:

- offer funerals at different price ranges (there's no need to spend more than is a comfortable outlay for you)
- dress the deceased if you wish them to wear anything special (such as a naval uniform, best suit or a favourite dress)

- contact the relevant minister or priest of the religion of your choice if you want a religious ceremony. (This is not a legal requirement although many families like to have a religious service. Civil celebrants also conduct funerals.)
- write funeral notices and place them in the newspaper for you
- supply the forms of registration of death, assist you in completing them and lodge them for you
- arrange for the body to be taken to their premises where it will be 'laid out' (the preferred term today is 'taken into the care of the funeral director') where it waits for burial or cremation
- provide a hearse for the body (a special car for the coffin), a driver and staff to carry the coffin
- provide transport for the chief mourners. (Black chauffeur-driven mourning cars may be hired, but many funeral directors are moving away from the use of mourning cars owing to their high cost.)
- arrange the presentation of the memorial booklet which contains the signatures of those who attended the funeral.

Many families like to use their own cars and form a cortege (a procession of cars) immediately behind the hearse on the way to the church, or hire a limousine (either a stretch or a sedan) from a local company. It is common to leave the headlights on to distinguish that you're part of a funeral procession.

If the family of the deceased, or the deceased themselves, has no funds to pay for the funeral, the family must firstly personally make application to the courthouse for a government-assisted funeral. If approved, this is handled by the Government Funeral Director Contractor.

How quickly should a funeral be conducted?
This will depend on how many friends or relatives from interstate or overseas may want to attend. Usually two or three days is considered appropriate.

How to write an obituary
Obituaries are written to 'sing the praises of the dead' and are often published in newspapers by the family of the deceased.

Often remembrance obituaries are published to mark the anniversary of a death and contain personal messages from the deceased's family or close friends.

SAMPLE OBITUARY

Sadly missed will be Mrs Edna Frammer of Maleny who is survived by her three children and her husband, Ted. For over thirty years Mrs Frammer has been a much loved and welcomed member of our community. She was a wonderful mother to Martha, Liz and Steve and an indulgent and loving grandmother to Tamara, Kim and Stacey. Her efforts in organising and maintaining Maleny's youth club and her donations annually to the school fete to raise funds for the school, will never be forgotten and nor shall she. A tribute to her greatness is that her three children survive her as pillars of the community, and we offer them our deepest sympathies in their time of sadness. Rest in peace Edna, and thank you.

What to wear to a funeral

Wearing black is no longer strictly observed at funerals today. Men are best to wear dark colours although a suit is unnecessary as long as the outfit is appropriate. Remember you're showing respect for the deceased and their family.

After the funeral

Many funeral homes now offer light refreshments in their chapels or adjacent rooms after a service, although a small fee may apply for this.

Regardless of where a 'wake' or post-funeral afternoon tea is held, this custom is particularly pleasant, especially if some of the mourners have had an early morning start to travel a long distance.

What do you do if you can't attend the funeral?

You should write a short letter of condolence as soon as you hear of the death. It should be natural and express how you feel—if you are unable to write then you should buy a 'card of condolence' and write a personal message on it.

Note of condolence

When sending a letter of condolence you need to state how sad you are to hear of the news, say something positive about the deceased, make an offer to help the grieving party or parties in any way and that you sympathise with them.

SAMPLE NOTE OF CONDOLENCE

Dear Fiona,

We cannot begin to say how shocked and saddened we are on hearing the news of your sister's sudden death.

Amanda was a wonderful wife and a caring mother and she will be much missed. Both Jim and I know what it's like to feel such a loss and how difficult it is for friends, like us, to find the right words to express sympathy for you at this time.

We hope you'll contact us if there's anything at all that we can do to help at this difficult time.

We want you to know that we are thinking of you and that we sympathise with your grief.

Sincerely,
Kerry and Jim Kelly

Chapter 10

TITLES AND FORMS OF ADDRESS

You may have occasion to associate with parliamentarians, dignitaries, royalty or military personnel in your lifetime, so it pays to know the correct way to address them and their correct title. A person's title indicates the honours or awards they have accumulated and can be prefixed or affixed, i.e. placed before or after their name. Honorary prefixed titles are given to royalty, while prefixed titles are also given to ecclesiastics, academics or others of professional distinction. Affixed titles (or postnominals) usually only consist of abbreviations or initials, however sometimes honorary affixed titles are given. The following should give you some idea of how to address Australia's VIPs.

ROYALTY
The Queen

The Queen's correct title in Australia is Elizabeth the Second, by the Grace of God Queen of Australia and Her other Realms and Territories, Head of the Commonwealth. She is referred to as 'Her Majesty, the Queen'.

When speaking you should address her first as 'Your Majesty', but subsequently as 'Ma'am'.

To send her a letter, address the envelope: Private Secretary to Her Majesty the Queen. You should conclude the letter with, 'I have the honour to remain [your full name]'.

Other members of the Royal Family

All other members of the Royal Family should be introduced as 'His/Her Royal Highness' [title].

When first spoken to they should be addressed as 'Your Royal Highness' and in further conversation as 'Sir' or 'Ma'am'.

Any correspondence should be addressed to 'His/Her Royal Highness, [title]'. For example, 'His Royal Highness, The Prince of Wales'.

VICEROYALTY
Governor-General
The Governor-General of Australia is introduced as 'The Governor-General of Australia, the Honourable Mr/Mrs/Ms [surname]'.

When spoken to they are referred to as 'Sir' or 'Ma'am'.

Any correspondence should be addressed to the 'Official Secretary at Government House'. The letter should open with 'Your Excellency'.

Governor (of a State)
The Governor of a State is introduced as 'His/Her Excellency, The Governor of [the State]'.

When speaking, you would address him or her as 'Your Excellency' and then as 'Sir' or 'Ma'am'.

Any correspondence should be addressed to 'His/Her Excellency, the Governor of [the State]'.

AMBASSADORS AND HIGH COMMISSIONERS
Ambassadors or High Commissioners are introduced as 'His/Her Excellency, the High Commissioner/Ambassador to [country]' (although this title is dropped when they retire). In the country of the ambassador's office, his or her spouse is also known as 'His/Her Excellency' in some cases.

When first spoken to they are addressed as 'Your Excellency' and then as 'Sir' or 'Ma'am'. Other consular or diplomatic staff are addressed only by their name and appointment. For example, 'Mr Henry Wong, Chief Consular Translator'.

Any correspondence should be addressed to 'His/Her Excellency, the High Commissioner/Ambassador of [country]'.

PARLIAMENTARIANS
The Prime Minister
The Prime Minister is introduced as 'The Honourable Dr/Mr/Mrs/Ms [full name], Prime Minister of Australia', e.g. 'The Honourable Mr John Howard, Prime Minister of Australia'.

When speaking to the Prime Minister you would address him or her as 'Dr/Mr/Mrs/Ms Prime Minister' or just 'Prime Minister'. In further conversation they are addressed as 'Sir', 'Ma'am' or 'Dr/Mr/Mrs/Ms Prime Minister'.

Any correspondence for the Prime Minister should be addressed to 'The Rt. Hon. [initial] [surname and postnominals] Prime Minister of the Commonwealth of Australia'. You should begin the letter with either 'Dear Sir/Madam' or 'Dear Mr/Mrs/Ms Prime Minister'.

The State Premier

The State Premier is introduced as 'The Honourable Dr/Mr/Mrs/Ms [full name], Premier of [the State]'. For example, 'The Honourable Mr Bob Carr, Premier of New South Wales'.

When speaking to the Premier you would address him/her as either 'Dr/Mr/Mrs/Ms [surname]' or just as 'Premier'. In further conversation they are addressed as 'Sir', 'Ma'am' or 'Dr/Mr/Mrs/Ms [surname]'.

To write a letter to the Premier, address the envelope to 'The Honourable Dr/Mr/Ms/Mrs [the Premier's full name] [any post-nominals] Premier of [the State]'. Open the letter with 'Dear Mr/Mrs/Ms [surname]'.

Federal or State ministers

Ministers in either Federal or State Governments take the title 'The Honourable', which is generally abbreviated to 'The Hon. Minister.'

When speaking, the respective Minister would be introduced as 'The Hon. Dr/Mr/Ms/Mrs [Minister's full name], MP, Minister for [portfolio]' and addressed as 'Sir', 'Ma'am' or 'Dr/Mr/Mrs/Ms [surname]'.

Address mail to 'The Hon. Dr/Mr/Ms/Mrs [full name] [postnominals], MP, Minister for [portfolio]'.

Senators

Senators are introduced as 'Senator the Honourable Dr/Mr/Mrs/Ms [full name], Minister for [portfolio]'. Senators are referred to simply as 'Senator [full name].'

When speaking, the Senator is introduced as 'Senator [surname]'.

When writing to the respective Senator, address the envelope to 'The Senator, Dr/Mr/Ms/Mrs [full name]'.

Note: Territories often bestow different prefixed honorific titles to members of the Legislative Assembly. As a result, ACT Ministers and the Speaker don't receive the title 'The Honourable'; instead they have their own preferred titles and you obtain a list of these from the assembly. While Ministers in the Northern Territory still take the title of 'The Honourable', the Administrator of the Northern Territory should be addressed as 'His/Her Honour the Administrator Mr/Ms/Mrs/Ms [full name]'.

LOCAL GOVERNMENT
Lord mayors
Lord Mayors are referred to as 'The Right Honourable'; however, this usually isn't applied to their name. The titles 'Alderman' or 'Councillor' are preferred, regardless of the Lord Mayor's sex, and dependant on the city in which the Lord Mayor holds office. The Lord Mayors of Brisbane, Hobart and Sydney are usually referred to as 'Alderman [full name]'; in Adelaide the Lord Mayor takes no title other than 'Dr/Mr/Mrs/Ms [full name]'; while in Melbourne the Lord Mayor is referred to as 'Councillor [full name]'. The Lord Mayors of Darwin, Newcastle and Wollongong are addressed as 'The Right Worshipful the Lord Mayor of [city]'. If the Lord Mayor is male, his wife is addressed as 'The Lady Mayoress of [city]'. You should address the Lord Mayor first as 'Lord Mayor' and subsequently as 'Sir/Madam'; and any correspondence should open with 'Dear Lord Mayor'.

Mayors
Mayors of most other Australian cities are introduced as 'His/Her Worship, the Mayor of [city]'. If the Mayor is male, his wife is addressed as 'The Mayoress of [city].'

JUDICIARY
Justices—High, federal, family and supreme courts
Justices should be referred to as 'Justice [surname]' and have the title of 'The Honourable Justice [full name] [postnominals]'.

When speaking, you would address him or her as 'Your Honour'. Outside of court, they are referred to as 'Justice [surname]' or 'Judge'.

When writing, address the envelope as 'The Honourable Justice [full name], Chief Justice of the High Court of Australia' and begin the letter with 'Dear Chief Justice'.

Judges—District courts

Judges have the title of 'The Honourable Judge [surname] [postnominals]'.

When speaking in court, you would call them 'Your Honour'. Outside of court, they are referred to as 'Judge [surname]'.

When writing you should address the envelope to 'His/ Her Honour Judge [surname] [postnominals], Judges' Chambers, [specific court, e.g. district, family]' and open the letter with 'Dear Judge' or 'Your Honour'.

Magistrates

Magistrates are referred to as 'His/Her Worship [full name] [postnominals]'.

When speaking in court, you would address them as 'His/Her Worship'. Outside of court you address them as 'The Honourable Magistrate [full name]'.

When writing, address the envelope to 'Magistrate [full name] [postnominals]', and open the letter with 'Dear Sir/Madam'.

Retired justices

In some cases retired justices retain the title 'The Hon.' before their names and in others they revert to 'Dr/Mr/Mrs/Ms.'

ECCLESIASTICS
Pope

The Pope should be introduced as 'His Holiness, Pope [papal name]'. He should be addressed as 'Your Holiness'.

Cardinal

A Cardinal is introduced as 'His Eminence, Cardinal [full name]'. He should then be addressed as 'Your Eminence'.

Archbishop

An archbishop should be introduced as 'His Grace, Archbishop [full name]'. He should then be addressed as 'Your Grace'.

Anglican minister

Anglican ministers will be introduced as 'The Reverend [full name]' and should be addressed as 'Mr [surname]' both in conversation and in writing.

Roman Catholic priest

A Catholic priest will be introduced as 'The Reverend Father [surname]' and should be addressed as 'Father [surname]'.

Greek Orthodox priest

A Greek Orthodox priest will be introduced as 'Reverend Father [surname]', and should be addressed as 'Father [surname]'.

Jewish rabbi

A Jewish rabbi will be introduced as 'Rabbi [surname]' and you should address them in the same way.

MILITARY PERSONNEL
Army

Most Australian army personnel, although introduced by their rank and full name, are addressed by their rank and their surname. This is the case for Generals, Brigadiers, Colonels, Majors and Captains, and most of those in the non-commissioned ranks (Warrant Officers, Regimental Sergeant Majors, Sergeant Majors, Staff Sergeants, Sergeants, Corporal/Bombadiers, Lance Corporal/Bombardiers). The exceptions are that Lieutenant Generals and Major Generals are addressed only as 'General [surname]', Lieutenant Colonels as 'Colonel [surname]' and Lieutenants or 2nd Lieutenants as 'Mr/Ms [surname]'. Privates, although introduced by their rank and surname, will be called only 'Private' in direct address.

Navy

Australian Navy personnel are also introduced by their rank and full name, but addressed by their rank and surname. For example, an Admiral would be introduced to you as 'Admiral [full name]' but you would call them only 'Admiral [surname]' when you spoke to them. This rule applies for Admirals, Vice Admirals, Rear Admirals, Commodores, Captains, Commanders, Lieutenant Commanders, Lieutenants, Sub-Lieutenants and Midshipman. Those in the non-commissioned ranks (Warrant Officers, Chief Petty Officers, Petty Officers, Leading Seaman/Able Seaman, Leading Wran, Senior Wran or Wran) are also introduced by their rank and full name, but are addressed only by their rank and surname. When writing to a female member in the Navy, do not write Wran after their rank.

Air Force

As with Australian Army and Navy personnel, Australian Air Force personnel are mostly introduced by their rank and full name, but addressed by their rank and surname. This applies for Air Marshals, Air Vice Marshals, Air Commodores, Group Captains, Wing Commanders, Squadron Leaders, Flight Lieutenants and Warrant Officers. The exceptions to this rule are Flying Officers and Pilot Officers, who are addressed as 'Mr/Mrs/Ms [surname]'. Those in the non-commissioned ranks (Flight Sergeants, Sergeants, Corporals, Leading Aircraftsmen/women and Aircraftsmen/women) are still introduced by their rank and full name, but addressed only but their rank and surname.

POLICE

In dealing with members of the police force, enquire as to their rank and address them accordingly.

HONOURS AND AWARDS

Honours and awards are indicated by their initial letters after the surname of the person. Only the main awards are listed below and further information can be obtained from the Protocol Department in the Premiers Office. The correct order is: orders, decorations, medals, distinctions and academic qualifications.

Common abbreviations

VC	Victoria Cross
GC	George Cross
CV	Cross of Valour
KG/LG	Knight/Lady of the Garter
KT/LT	Knight/Lady of the Thistle
GCB	Knight/Dame Grand Cross of the Order of the Bath
OM	Order of Merit
AK/AD	Knight/Dame of the Order of Australia
GCMG	Knight/Dame Grand Cross of the order of St Michael and St George
GCVO	Knight/Dame Grand Cross of the Royal Victorian Order
GBE	Knight/Dame Grand Cross of the Order of the British Empire
AC	Companion of the Order of Australia
CH	Companion of Honour
KCB/DCB	Knight/Dame of the Order of the Bath
KCMG/DCMG	Knight/Dame Commander of the Order of St Michael and St George
KCVO/DVCO	Knight/Dame Commander of the Royal Victorian Order
KBE/DBE	Knight/Dame Commander of the Order of the British Empire
KB	Knight Bachelor
AO	Officer of the Order of Australia
CB	Companion of the Order of the Bath
CMG	Companion of the Order of St Michael and St George
CVO	Commander of the Royal Victorian Order
CBE	Commander of the Order of the British Empire
SG	Star of Gallantry

SC	Star of Courage
DSO	Distinguished Service Order
DSC	Distinguished Service Cross
AM	Member of the Order of Australia
LVO	Lieutenant of the Royal Victorian Order
OBE	Officer of the Order of the British Empire
ISO	Companion of the Imperial Service Order
MVO	Member of the Royal Victorian Order
MBE	Member of the Order of the British Empire
CSC	Conspicuous Service Cross
NSC	Nursing Service Cross
DSC	Distinguished Service Cross
MC	Military Cross
DFC	Distinguished Flying Cross
AFC	Air Force Cross
MG	Medal for Gallantry
BM	Bravery Medal
DSM	Distinguished Service Medal
PSM	Public Service Medal
APM	Australian Police Medal
AFSM	Australian Fire Service Medal
OAM	Medal of the Order of Australia
DCM	Distinguished Conduct Medal
CGM	Conspicuous Gallantry Medal
GM	George Medal
CSM	Conspicuous Service Medal
QPM	Queen's Police Medal for Gallantry
QFSM	Queen's Fire Service Medal for Gallantry
DSM	Distinguished Service Medal
MM	Military Medal
DFM	Distinguished Flying Medal
AFM	Air Force Medal
QGM	Queen's Gallantry Medal
RVM	Royal Victorian Medal
BEM	British Empire Medal

INDEX

OTHER BOOKS BY PATSY ROWE

No Sweat Not To Worry, She'll Be Jake

When Patsy Rowe decided to build her first house she thought she could leave it all up to the builders—after all, they were the experts. However, the five months she spent as site supervisor on the house were fraught with traumas, frustrations and confrontations. She did sweat and she did worry because, inevitably, it was never Jake.

But Patsy took it all in her stride and never lost her sense of humour. *No Sweat Not to Worry, She'll be Jake* is a light-hearted and even affectionate look at the building industry.

Am I Having Fun Yet?

Imagine—you've just finished building your dream home. You've endured the traumas and frustrations of dealing with tradesmen whom you've had to cajole, bribe and beg in order to get your home finished.

Suddenly you are married and five of your husband's children, two grandchildren, a stepson-in-law and an assortment of animals are living with you. By the end of the year your cosy two-bedroom dream home has turned into a six-bedroom mansion.

Am I Having Fun Yet? is a factional story of the comical incidents from Patsy's first year of marriage to Bill, a psychiatrist. She tells of her trials with various tradesmen, her marriage celebrant, her nosy neighbour, her husband's patients, her stepchildren and her in-laws.

You ARE Leaving Tuesday, Aren't You?

You may think you've heard it all before—the domestic tribulations of setting the VCR, dealing with selectively-deaf tradesmen and trying to cope with self-invited house guests … But when it comes from the pen of indefatigable and generally unflappable Patsy Rowe, it's a giggle-a-minute look at life as a home handywoman, amateur veterinarian and hostess extraordinaire.

In these 27 breezy tales of life, Patsy, chardonnay in one hand, Ventolin in the other—survives it all, from primadonna poodles and paranoid passengers to pre-natal lorikeets.

Manners for the Millennium—Etiquette for Men and Women

Manners for the Millennium—Etiquette for Men and Women is the complete reference to everyday etiquette and coping in any social situation. The book details how to announce your engagement and plan your wedding and reception, whether you're Anglican, Catholic, Greek Orthodox, Jewish or non-religious; ten things to talk about on a first or blind date; how to make small talk and become a champion conversationalist; tips for easy, elegant entertaining—with tips on food and wine matching; eight tips on serving wine; naming and baptising new arrivals, and dealing with divorce and death. Includes sample recipes, wedding invitations, obituaries, wedding speeches and toasts, thank you notes and much, much more.

Business Etiquette—Achieving a Competitive Edge in Business

To get to the top of the business or professional world means gaining an extra edge. *Business Etiquette* provides the strategies to achieve success by detailing what to do, when to do it, and how to do it. You'll discover how to dress for success for job interviews or business; how to walk into a room full of strangers, mix, mingle and initiate small talk; how to update your dining etiquette and entertain for business; how to entertain and impress international clients; how to write impressive business letters, résumés, speeches and toasts, oral reports and references, with samples to illustrate.

Secret Women's Business—How to Get It All and Keep It

How can the modern woman achieve all her dreams? How can she have it all ... a successful career, a happy marriage and a functional family ... and keep it? *Secret Women's Business* uncovers the various challenges facing women today—love, lust, money, power, passion and loss—and shows you how to combine all the elements of your life, whatever your age, with your innermost dreams and desires. Inside you'll find tricks on juggling priorities with play, the secrets of successful businesswomen, how to win at the dating game, achieving greater intimacy in your relationships, how to discover your 'self' and self-acceptance.

ABOUT THE AUTHOR

Patsy Rowe is the author of three books on today's etiquette for men and women. She travels around Australia and overseas speaking on business etiquette at more than 100 corporate engagements each year. She is on Radio 2UE in Sydney, and is a regular guest on the ABC and on Radio Pacific in New Zealand. Patsy conducts corporate in-house seminars on business etiquette covering topics such as how to 'work a room', initiate small talk, thank a speaker and say a few words through to perfecting dining etiquette. These previously neglected life skills are being seen by corporations today to be able to help participants to cope with social and business situations in a more confident manner. Her Boot Camps for Blokes is a seminar tailored especially for men when wives, girlfriends and mothers entrust their blokes to Patsy for a day of spit 'n' polish. In 1986, Patsy was invited by the Minister of Consumer Affairs to join the Board of the Building Services Corporation where she was the first woman ever appointed to sit as a judge hearing cases against builders who over-charged or refused to complete a contract. Her latest venture is teaching etiquette on the School of the Air. For more information on Patsy, go to her websites at:

www.etiquette.com.au
www.secretwomensbusiness.net